P9-DOC-100

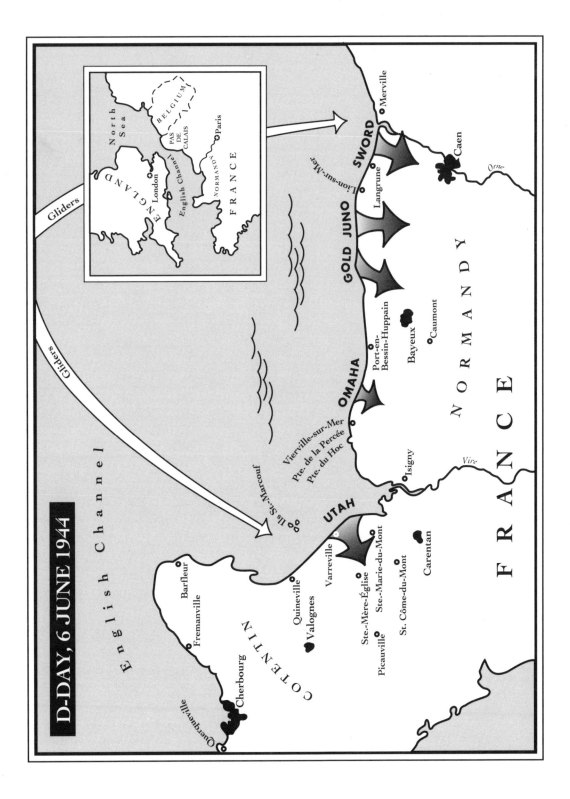

D-DAY, 6 JUNE 1944

English Channel

Gliders

Gliders

ENGLAND
North Sea
London
English Channel
BELGIUM
PAS DE CALAIS
Paris
NORMANDY
FRANCE

SWORD
Merville
Caen
Orne
Langrune
Lion-sur-Mer
GOLD JUNO
Port-en-Bessin-Huppain
Bayeux
Caumont
OMAHA
Vierville-sur-Mer
Pte. de la Percée
Pte. du Hoc
Isigny
Vire
Îls St.-Marcouf
UTAH
Varreville
Ste.-Marie-du-Mont
St. Côme-du-Mont
Carentan
NORMANDY
FRANCE

COTENTIN
Barfleur
Fremanville
Quineville
Valognes
Ste.-Mère-Église
Picauville
Cherbourg
Querqueville

D-DAY NORMANDY

Also by the Authors:

The Way It Was: Pearl Harbor—The Original Photographs (1991)

by Donald M. Goldstein and Katherine V. Dillon

The Williwaw War (1992)

The Pearl Harbor Papers: Inside the Japanese Plans (1993)

(with Gordon W. Prange)

At Dawn We Slept: The Untold Story of Pearl Harbor (1981)

Miracle at Midway (1982)

Target Tokyo: The Story of the Sorge Spy Ring (1984)

Pearl Harbor: The Verdict of History (1987)

December 7, 1941: The Day the Japanese Attacked Pearl Harbor (1988)

God's Samurai: Lead Pilot at Pearl Harbor (1990)

(with Masataka Chihaya)

Fading Victory: The Diary of Admiral Matome Ugaki (1991)

by J. Michael Wenger and Robert J. Cressman

Steady Nerves and Stout Hearts: The Enterprise (CV-6) Air Group at Pearl Harbor, 7 December 1941 (1989)

Infamous Day: The Marines at Pearl Harbor, 7 December 1941 (1992)

D-DAY NORMANDY

THE STORY AND PHOTOGRAPHS

DONALD M. GOLDSTEIN, KATHERINE V. DILLON
Coauthors of *At Dawn We Slept* and *Miracle at Midway*
and J. MICHAEL WENGER

Brassey's (US)

A Maxwell Macmillan Company

Washington • New York • London

Book design and production by
Yaron Fidler

Brassey's (US)

Editorial Offices
Brassey's (US)
8000 Westpark Drive
First Floor
McLean, Virginia 22102

Order Department
Brassey's Book Orders
c/o Macmillan Publishing Co.
100 Front Street, Box 500
Riverside, New Jersey 08075

Brassey's (US) is a Maxwell Macmillan Company. Brassey's books are available at special discounts for bulk purchases for sales promotions, premiums, fund-raising, or educational use through the Special Sales Director, Macmillan Publishing Company, 866 Third Avenue, New York, New York 10022.

Library of Congress Cataloging-in-Publication Data
Goldstein, Donald M.
D-Day Normandy : the story and photographs / by Donald M.
Goldstein, Katherine V. Dillon, and J. Michael Wenger.
p. cm.
Includes bibliographical references and index.
ISBN 0-02-881057-0
1. World War, 1939–1945—Campaigns—France—Normandy—Pictorial works. 2. Normandy (France)—History, Military—Pictorial works.
I. Dillon, Katherine V. II. Wenger, J. Michael. III. Title.
D756.5.N6G65   1994   93-35473
   940.54'214—dc20   CIP

10 9 8 7 6 5 4 3 2 1

Printed in the United States of America

Foreword

Half a century has passed and two generations have been born since Americans said their goodbyes and boarded ships and planes for battles that would determine the world's future. Few knew that many of them would soon be part of the largest invasion force in history. On D-Day, 6 June 1944, the Allies stormed the beaches of Normandy, marking the turning point of the war in Europe and ultimately leading to the destruction of Hitler's Third Reich.

As the fiftieth anniversary of that watershed event approaches, the Battle of Normandy Foundation, a nonprofit organization founded in 1985, brings to the American people its mission of honoring veterans and keeping alive the ideals and lessons of World War II. This effort is being carried out with the support of veterans, private citizens, and corporations.

In 1990, members of the U.S. Congress formed the 50th Anniversary Commission and encouraged the Battle of Normandy Foundation to coordinate a private-sector initiative honoring the American men and women who served in the European theater of operations, thereby informing Americans of the contributions and sacrifices World War II veterans made to rekindle the torch of freedom and restore human rights to Europe.

As part of this effort, the Battle of Normandy Foundation is proud to present *D-Day Normandy: The Story and Photographs* as its official fiftieth-anniversary commemorative volume.

An AUSA Book

The Association of the United States Army, or AUSA, was founded in 1950 as a not-for-profit organization dedicated to education concerning the role of the U.S. Army, to providing material for military professional development, and to the promotion of proper recognition and appreciation of the profession of arms. Its constituencies include those who serve in the Army today, including Army National Guard, Army Reserve, and Army civilians, and the retirees and veterans who have served in the past, and all their families. A large number of public-minded citizens and business leaders are also an important constituency. The Association seeks to educate the public, elected and appointed officials, and leaders of defense industry on crucial issues involving the adequacy of our national defense, particularly those issues affecting land warfare.

In 1988 AUSA established within its existing organization a new entity known as the Institute of Land Warfare. Its purpose is to extend the educational work of AUSA by sponsoring scholarly publications, to include books, monographs, and essays on key defense issues, as well as workshops and symposia. Among the volumes chosen for designation as "An AUSA Institute of Land Warfare Book" are both new texts and reprints of titles of enduring value that are no longer in print. Topics include history, policy issues, strategy, and tactics. Publication as an AUSA Book does not indicate that the Association of the United States Army and the publisher agree with everything in the book, but does suggest that the AUSA and the publisher believe this book will stimulate the thinking of AUSA members and others concerned about important issues.

Contents

Preface

Soon after *The Way It Was: Pearl Harbor* was published, Frank Margiotta of Brassey's (US) decided to put out a similar book covering one of the greatest military operations in history. He allotted the task to us—the same team that produced *The Way It Was*.

As with the previous project, we had many photographs to choose from, and again the problem was deciding what to use and what—reluctantly—to set aside. We were struck anew by the fact that photography gives the historian an entirely new dimension beyond the written record and oral testimony. What would one not give for a similar record of, say, the battles of Yorktown or Waterloo?

We have divided this book into nine chapters. Chapter 1, "The Antagonists," introduces the key American, British, and German personnel; chapter 2, "Men and Machines," briefly describes the arms, artillery, tanks, aircraft, and ships employed; chapter 3, "Rehearsal, Training, and Preparation," discusses the Allies' long, hard preparations that took place in Great Britain; chapter 4, "Loading Operations and Cross-Channel Voyage," sees the men and matériel loaded on board ships and safely transported to the Normandy coast; chapter 5, "D-Day: 6 June 1944," depicts the action on D-Day; chapter 6, "Allied Buildup and Consolidation," takes the story beyond the initial beachheads; chapter 7, "Cherbourg," briefly describes the taking of the major port of Cherbourg; chapter 8, "Aftermath," covers some of the post-battle events; and chapter 9, "Epilogue," provides glimpses of the cost of victory with scenes of the Allies' burials and cemeteries. The theme throughout this entire volume is people—generals and admirals, soldiers and sailors, civilian dignitaries and average citizens.

A pictorial history of this type is necessarily limited in scope, so we have chosen to portray the American military action exclusively. Nor could we include the activities of all U.S. units engaged. Much else was going on—the British landings in Normandy, high-level political and strategic discussions and planning among the Allies in England, and the fascinating story of German efforts and frustrations. We hope this book will whet the appetite for more information on this subject, and we would like to recommend a few books that should prove helpful: H. H. Arnold, *Global Mission*; Omar N. Bradley, *A Soldier's Story*; Winston S. Churchill, *The Second World War*, Vol. V, *Closing the Ring*, and Vol. VI, *Triumph and Tragedy*; David Eisenhower, *Eisenhower at War: 1943–1945*; Dwight D. Eisenhower, *Crusade in Europe*; B. L. Montgomery, *The Memoirs of Field Marshal the Viscount Montgomery of Alamein, K.G.*; Samuel Eliot Morison, *History of United States Naval Operations in World War II*, Vol. XI, *The Invasion of France and Germany*; and Cornelius Ryan, *The Longest Day*. Of course, many, many other books are available, but these will give a good overall view and, not too incidentally, are good reads.

Throughout this book we have followed certain conventions such as using the twenty-four-hour clock, according to military custom, to prevent confusion between A.M. and P.M. With the photographs, occasionally a contemporary print of an individual was not available, so the rank insignia may not be the one that the man wore on D-Day. Abbreviations are those used in 1944. Finally, a list of German ranks and their U.S. Army equivalents is found at the end of the book.

We hope *D-Day Normandy* will give the reader some concept of what was involved in the early stages of the invasion that eventually freed Europe.

We would like to dedicate this book to the memory of those who died in that great campaign.

Acknowl-
edgments

This book would have been impossible without the cooperation of many people. We would like to acknowledge our debt to James Enos, Nathan Herman, David MacIsaac, Kendall Stanley, Anita Tilford, and Willadean Bailey. We also thank Robert J. Cressman, Charles Haberlein, and Kathy Lloyd of the Naval Historical Center and Dale Connelly and Sharon Culley of the National Archives. Special thanks go to our friends at Brassey's (US)—Don McKeon, Frank Margiotta, and Vicki Chamlee—for their technical advice and encouragement; to Yaron Fidler, our designer; and to all the hard-working and dedicated people at the following organizations who never really get their just credit:

Air War College
Army War College
German Bundesarchiv
National Archives
Naval Historical Center

Goldstein and Wenger would like to pay a special tribute to their wives—Mariann and Mary Ann, respectively—for their patience over the long haul.

DONALD M. GOLDSTEIN, PH.D.
Professor of Public and International Affairs
University of Pittsburgh
Pittsburgh, Pennsylvania

KATHERINE V. DILLON
CWO, USAF (Ret.)
Arlington, Virginia

J. MICHAEL WENGER, M.A.
Raleigh, North Carolina

Introduction

When Japan precipitated the Pacific War on 7 December 1941, it presented the Allies with a fresh set of problems. On the one hand, they faced the almost certain loss of their Asian possessions. On the other hand, Japan had brought in the United States, which the Allies in general believed tipped the scales toward their inevitable eventual victory. They maintained that the Pacific would have to take second priority. For the United States, the question was not that simple. Unlike the European powers, the United States had a long coastline on the Pacific. Moreover, public opinion, enraged by Pearl Harbor, would not permit mere token resistance against Japanese aggression. Furthermore, the United States was not yet ready militarily to take on two major wars at once.

However, Washington had decided upon a "Germany first" strategy, and despite heavy pressure, President Franklin D. Roosevelt stood by the decision. From the first, all concerned understood that eventually the Allies must invade Europe; in no other way could the entrenched, well-armed, and highly skilled Germans be defeated decisively. Plans for Operation Bolero, which became the foundation for Operation Overlord, were under way by the spring of 1942, but an all-out, frontal assault across the English Channel was out of the question at that time.

Thus the first major U.S. participation in the war against Adolf Hitler was Operation Torch, the invasion of North Africa, with Gen. Dwight D. ("Ike") Eisenhower in command. The conquest of Sicily and the surrender of Italy followed. All of these campaigns took a very long time and proceeded to the accompaniment of a barrage of the Kremlin's demands for a second front into the heart of the continent instead of moving along the edges. Joseph Stalin believed, with considerable reason, that the Soviet Union had been bearing the brunt against Hitler.

By 1943 the British and Americans had decided to begin training for Overlord. Once again, after much debate, it was decided that an American would command. After hovering for some time between Gen. George C. Marshall and Eisenhower, Roosevelt settled upon Ike. This time, by sheer force of numbers, the Americans would be the dominant force; heretofore, theirs had been a supporting role for the British. Sectors of the Normandy coast, with picturesque code names, were assigned: Sword and Gold to the British, Juno to the Canadians, Utah and Omaha to the Americans.

Of course, the arrival in Great Britain of over a million young Americans and untold tons of equipment did not escape the attention of the Germans charged with defending Fortress Europe. But the Germans were far from unanimous as to how this should be done. Field Marshal Gerd von Rundstedt proposed to let the invaders land and move off the beaches, where the Germans could engage them on terrain more suitable for the employment of troops and armament. Gen. Erwin Rommel preferred to stop the invasion on the beaches before it had the chance to entrench itself.

Rommel received the assignment of defending the coast, and he took up his duties with his usual skill and vigor. He had truly formidable beach obstacles emplaced and worked out many technical improvements. Rommel was not present on D-Day. Informed that the weather would prohibit a cross-Channel invasion for at least two weeks, he took off by car for Obersalzburg to confer with Hitler.

The German meteorologists were mistaken. Their instruments did not detect the brief break in the weather that made Overlord possible on 6 June.

For those who lived through World War II, particularly if not in combat, D-Day holds a special place. Pearl Harbor was a day of wrath; VE-Day and VJ-Day were days of joy; but D-Day was a day of prayer. Instinctively everyone in the free world, from the highest to the humblest, realized that this operation had nothing to do with such forces as politics, economics, or the balance of power; it was the start of a crusade—the war's last great campaign against the forces of evil. In London, ceremonies were held in St. Paul's Cathedral and Westminster Abbey. When the news reached the East Coast of the United States in the very early morning, many shift workers slipped into the nearest church for a brief prayer before going home. An impromptu prayer meeting in Madison Square Garden drew thousands.

Roosevelt scheduled his second fireside chat of the day—less than twenty-four hours before, he had announced the fall of Rome. To maintain the fiction that this invasion was not the primary operation, he had rejected widespread pleas for proclaiming "a single day of special prayer." But he ended his chat with a moving petition that could have left little doubt in the minds of German Intelligence, if a representative happened to be listening, of the importance of what was going on:

Almighty God: Our sons, pride of our nation, this day have set upon a mighty endeavor, a struggle to preserve our Republic, our religion and our civilization, and to set free a suffering humanity. . . .

They will need Thy blessings. Their road will be long and hard. . . . Success may not come with rushing speed, but . . . we know that by Thy grace, and by the righteousness of our cause, our sons will triumph. . . .

This is the story of that "mighty endeavor."

1-1. President Franklin D. Roosevelt signs the American declaration of war in December 1941. His arm band denotes mourning for his mother, who had died that autumn. Note Sam Rayburn's signature on the declaration.

1-2. King George VI, in admiral's uniform, makes an inspection tour of the heavy cruiser USS *Augusta* (CA-31) at Portland, England, just after 1400 on 25 May 1944. Note camouflage paint on the barrels of *Augusta*'s main battery.

CHAPTER 1 | The Antagonists

From the moment that President Franklin D. Roosevelt (FDR) signed the declaration of war (1-1), something in the nature of Overlord was readily predictable. The "Germany first" strategy had been adopted, and it was obvious that only a major invasion could free Europe from the deeply entrenched Nazis. Despite much public clamor to go all out against the Japanese, Roosevelt and the U.S. military leaders wisely kept to the Europe first strategy.

The president of the United States was both chief of state and head of the government. In Great Britain these two functions—which indeed can demand very different qualities of mind and character—are divided. During World War II, chief of state was King George VI (1-2). Throughout the war, he and Queen Elizabeth provided an irreproachable example of leadership. They remained at their posts of duty, sharing the hardships and dangers suffered by their people. As D-Day drew near, King George visited Portsmouth on 24 May. The next day he visited Portland, boarding USS *Augusta* at 1300 with Admirals Sir Bertram Ramsay, John L. Hall, and John Wilkes, and then ate lunch aboard the ship. At 1405 he inspected the ship with the above officers and Rear Adm. Alan G. Kirk.

Great Britain's head of government was Prime Minister Winston S. Churchill (1-3), one of history's prime examples of the "hour producing the man." For years Churchill

1-3. Winston S. Churchill, prime minister of Great Britain (*center, front row*), attends a conference with President Roosevelt. Adm. Ernest J. King is at far left in the front row, and Adm. Lord Louis Mountbatten stands between Churchill and FDR.

had been reviled and mocked as a "warmonger" and a throwback to the nineteenth century for insisting that Adolf Hitler and his Nazis were evil, and dangerous, and must be stopped. With the debacle following Munich, the British remembered the "prophet in his own country" and returned Churchill to the government, initially as first lord of the admiralty, then as prime minister. Now to the free world he symbolized Great Britain—her endurance, resistance, determination, and valor. During the long planning stages, he had reservations about Overlord, as did many British high-ranking officers. This was only natural. They still had vivid memories of World War I—the long-drawn-out horror, misery, and appalling loss of life involved in trench warfare.

Adm. Lord Louis Mountbatten played no direct role in Overlord, having been appointed supreme commander, Southeast Asia Command, in late August 1943. However, he once was chief of the Combined Operations Organization, charged with developing, among other things, techniques for amphibious landings. Churchill, Marshall, and others acknowledged Overlord's debt to Mountbatten's organization.

It was agreed that the commander of the invasion forces should be an American. For some time Roosevelt delayed the selection, hovering between Chief of Staff George C. Marshall and Gen. Dwight D. ("Ike") Eisenhower (1-4). Finally he decided that Marshall, with his experience and grasp of the overall picture, must remain in Washington, while Ike as a tested theater commander should head Overlord. The decision proved wise; Marshall was invaluable at headquarters and Ike was just the man for Overlord.

The three principal commanders directly under Ike

1-4. Gen. Dwight D. Eisenhower, commander, Supreme Allied Command, Allied Expeditionary Force. This photo was taken in 1945 after Ike received his fifth star.

1-5. Gen. Sir Bernard L. Montgomery, commander in chief of land forces, Allied Expeditionary Force, and commander in chief, Twenty-first Army Group. The Second British Army and First Canadian Army were also under his command. This photo shows Monty sitting in an M-5 Grant tank in North Africa.

1-6. Lt. Gen. Omar N. Bradley, commander, American Ground Forces *(left)*, meets Gen. George C. Marshall, chief of staff, U.S. Army *(center)*, and Gen. Henry H. ("Hap") Arnold, commander, USAAF *(right)*, on 12 June 1944 in Normandy. Note the barrage balloon above and SP (Shore Patrol) in background at left.

were British, which could have caused problems, but Ike had deep respect for the British people and their customs. He insisted to his military staff that the influx of thousands of young Americans in Great Britain be as little disruptive as possible. Plans and preparations for Overlord were already enormously complicated; moreover, Ike had to control and get the best out of such prima donnas as Gen. Sir Bernard L.("Monty") Montgomery (1-5).

Monty had a brilliant military record, dating back to World War I. When World War II began, he commanded the 3d Division in France. After escaping Dunkirk, he assumed command of the V Corps. During 1942–43 he led the British Eighth Army in Africa, Egypt, Sicily, and Italy. While in Africa, he achieved fame for defeating Rommel and his *Afrika Korps.*

Monty possessed a towering ego. He made no secret of the fact that he believed he should be in command of Overlord, with Ike kicked upstairs to some vague supervisory post.

Probably the best known of Ike's subordinate American commanders was Lt. Gen. Omar N. Bradley (1-6). He was Eisenhower's classmate at West Point, class of 1915. Bradley's pre–World War II career, like Ike's, had given little indication of his potential, although General Marshall had spotted him as promising while Bradley was an instructor at the Infantry School at Fort Benning, Georgia. Bradley could be very sensitive, but normally he conveyed the impression of down-to-earth practicality. His enlisted men thought the world of him, and he became known as "the GI general." Bradley had preceded Maj. Gen. Matthew B. Ridgway in command of the 82d Division, before it converted to Airborne. On 23 October 1943, the First Army under Bradley took over operational command of ground

forces in Great Britain. At the same time, the VII Corps was assigned to the First Army.

Another old friend of Ike's was Maj. Gen. Leonard T. Gerow (1-7). They had served together in 1916 at San An-

1-7. Maj. Gen. Leonard T. Gerow, commanding general, U.S. V Corps *(center)*, sits with Maj. Gen. Clarence R. Huebner, commander, 1st Infantry Division *(left)*, and with the commander of his shore party, Brig. Gen. W. M. Hoge *(right)*. This photo was taken aboard the USS *Ancon* (AGC-4) on 5 June 1944. *Ancon* was the amphibious force flagship for Assault Force "O." "Big Red 1" (the 1st Infantry Division) would bear the brunt of fighting on Omaha Beach.

1-8. Maj. Gen. J. Lawton Collins, commanding general, VII Corps.

1-10. Maj. Gen. Matthew B. Ridgway, commanding general, 82d Airborne Division *(left)*, confers with his assistant, Brig. Gen. James A. Gavin. This photo, showing Gavin as a major general, was taken on 20 January 1945, near the close of the Ardennes campaign.

1-9. Maj. Gen. Raymond O. Barton addresses troops of the 22d Infantry Regiment in July 1944 following the fall of Cherbourg.

1-11. Maj. Gen. Maxwell D. Taylor, commanding general, 101st Airborne Division.

tonio and ten years later were classmates at the Command and General Staff School at Fort Leavenworth, Kansas, where, according to Ike's grandson David, Eisenhower graduated first in their class by less than .001 of a point over Gerow. The latter had the bad luck to be chief of the War Department's War Plans Division when the Japanese struck Pearl Harbor on 7 December 1941. Four days later, Ike reported as Gerow's assistant and replaced him on 16 April 1942. The Army Pearl Harbor Board criticized Gerow, and his career suffered somewhat in consequence.

Unlike Eisenhower, Bradley, and Gerow, Maj. Gen. J. Lawton Collins (1-8) was a veteran of the Pacific War. As commander of the 25th Division in 1942–43, he had racked up a notable combat record in the Guadalcanal and New Georgia campaigns. He assumed command of the VII Corps in February 1944.

Of Eisenhower's division commanders, Maj. Gen. Raymond O. Barton (1-9) had been associated with the 4th Infantry Division since 1940, when he was its chief of staff. In June 1942 he assumed command of the 4th Motorized Division, which became the 4th Division. He arrived with his unit in the European theater of operations (ETO) in January 1944. He and his men were scheduled to seize Utah Beach.

In March 1942, Major General Ridgway (1-10) was assistant to Bradley in command of the 82d Division and became its commander in June 1942. After the 82d Division reorganized as the 82d Airborne Division, he remained in command throughout the Sicily and Italy campaigns.

Brig. Gen. James M. Gavin commanded the 505th Parachute Infantry Regiment of the 82d Airborne in July 1942. He led the regiment in the Sicily campaign and the Salerno drop in September 1943. He became assistant division commander under Ridgway in October 1943.

1-12. Brig. Gen. Anthony McAuliffe, assistant commander, 101st Airborne Division.

Maj. Gen. Maxwell D. Taylor (1-11) had been chief of staff of the 82d Division under Bradley. In 1943, he became artillery commander of the 82d Airborne. After serving in Sicily and Italy, he assumed command of the 101st Airborne in March 1944.

Seldom does a man go down in history for uttering a single word. Brig. Gen. Anthony McAuliffe (1-12), assistant commander of the 101st Airborne Division, achieved this distinction later during the Bastogne incident, when he responded to the suggestion that he surrender with a laconic "Nuts!" Some speculate that his actual reply was something considerably stronger, but that homely "Nuts!" struck a responsive chord with the American public.

1-13. Lt. Gen. George S. Patton, commanding general, U.S. Third Army, standing in a Dodge 3/4-ton command vehicle as he confers with one of his officers in Sicily, 1943.

1-14. Adm. Sir Bertram Ramsay, RN, commander in chief, naval forces, Allied Expeditionary Forces (left), strolls with Rear Adm. John L. Hall, commander, Task Force 124 (Assault Force "O"—Omaha Beach). Taken aboard *Ancon*, 24 May 1944.

Lt. Gen. George S. Patton (1-13) figured in the Normandy campaign only as part of the ruse intended to make the Germans think the invasion would come at Pas-de-Calais. Patton was given a dummy headquarters near Dover for his "First Army Group." Great numbers of landing craft appeared in the Thames and Medway rivers. Smoke from cooking fires, bogus radio traffic, and deserted tent cities aided in the deception, which succeeded beyond all imagining, keeping the German Fifteenth Army (nineteen divisions) pinned down at Calais. In his own spectacular fashion, Patton was quite as egocentric as Monty was in his dour way. Patton did not relish this inactive role, but he could look forward to commanding the Third Army in the near future.

For the invasion, the U.S. Navy at Normandy took its orders from Admiral Ramsay, Royal Navy (RN) (1-14). Rear Admiral Hall described him as "quiet, brilliant, intelligent, determined, and easy to get along with." He had retired as a rear admiral in 1938 and was later recalled to active service. He served as flag officer, Dover, and as such was a key player in the Dunkirk evacuation. Then he became chief naval planner for Operation Torch (the invasion of North Africa), working closely with Ike. Ramsay's Overlord command was divided into two primary parts—the Western Naval Task Force (mostly U.S. Navy) supporting the American troops under Bradley and the Eastern Naval Force (mostly Royal Navy) supporting British and Canadian troops.

At the outbreak of World War II in Europe, Rear Admiral Kirk (1-15) had been naval attaché at the U.S. Embassy in London. Then in 1942, he had served as chief of

1-15. Rear Adm. Alan G. Kirk, commander, Task Force 122, Western Naval Force, watching the Normandy landings from his flagship, *Augusta*.

1-16. Rear Adm. Donald P. Moon, commander, Task Force 125 (Assault Force "U"—Utah Beach). Photo taken at Algiers on 24 March 1944.

staff for Adm. Harold R. ("Betty") Stark, commander of U.S. naval forces in Europe. In these capacities, he had become well acquainted with British customs and personalities. Later he became commander, Amphibious Forces, Atlantic Fleet, and led the assault on the eastern flank in the Sicily operation. He was on his thirty-ninth year of service when he returned to England to become overall U.S. naval commander for Overlord. His command embarked Bradley's First Army.

Rear Adm. Donald P. Moon (1-16), a dedicated and conscientious officer, had served aboard the battleship *Arizona* during World War I. There he invented new devices for plotting and fire control. At the outbreak of World War II,

he commanded Destroyer Squadron 8 of the Atlantic Fleet. He also played a major role in Operation Torch, later commanding an amphibious force in the Mediterranean. In January 1944, he was promoted to rear admiral to command Force "U," which supported the Utah Beach landing. His flagship was the *Bayfield* (APA-33); his force embarked the 4th Infantry Division and elements of VII Corps. Under the strain of command, he committed suicide 5 August 1944.

Rear Adm. Morton L. Deyo's (1-17) Bombardment Group for Force "U" included the heavy cruisers *Tuscaloosa* and *Quincy* (CA-71) and the battleship *Nevada* (BB-36). This force provided fire cover for the Utah landings and would shell any strong point offering opposition.

1-17. Rear Adm. Morton L. Deyo, commander, Force "U" Bombardment Group *(right)*, with Kirk *(center)*, and Ike *(left)*, 19 May 1944, on board *Tuscaloosa* (CA-37).

1-18. Rear Adm. John L. Hall, commander, Task Force 124 (Assault Force "O"), shown on his flagship, *Ancon*, in the English Channel, June 1944.

1-19. Rear Adm. Carlton F. Bryant, commander, Force "O" Bombardment Group. This photo was taken in December 1950.

1-20. Commodore Campbell D. Edgar, commander, Task Force 126 (Follow-up Force "B"—Omaha Beach). In this photo he is a captain in command of the transport USS *William P. Biddle* (APA-15) about 1941.

The naval commanders assigned to the landings on Omaha Beach were just as capable and experienced as their colleagues at Utah. Rear Admiral John L. Hall (**1-18**) supervised shipboard training in both Forces "U" and "O." He had more amphibious assault experience than any other American flag officer. He was very competent, calm, and self-controlled. Two days before the invasion, he stated, "I do not expect to be repulsed on any beach." His force embarked the 16th Regiment of the 1st Division, the 15th and 16th regiments of the 19th Division, the 2d and 5th Ranger battalions, and elements of V Corps.

Rear Adm. Carlton F. Bryant's (**1-19**) Bombardment Group for Force "O," which would cover the Omaha landings, included the battleship *Texas* (BB-35) and *Arkansas* (BB-33). Later a French admiral said, "To be under Admiral Bryant was a blessing for us."

During the North Africa campaign, Commodore Campbell D. Edgar (**1-20**) commanded Transport Division 5, earning the Distinguished Service Medal. Later he was awarded two Legion of Merit awards for his role in the invasions of Sicily and Italy. His flagship for TF 126 was *Maloy* (DE-791); his force embarked the balance of the 1st and 29th Infantry divisions, V Corps, and Engineer special units.

The success—indeed, the feasibility—of Overlord would depend in large measure upon pre-invasion softening-

1-21. Gen. Henry H. ("Hap") Arnold, commander, U.S. Army Air Force.

1-22. General Eisenhower *(left)* inspects a Ninth Air Force fighter base in March 1944, accompanied by Maj. Gen. Lewis H. Brereton, commanding general, Ninth Air Force *(right)*, and Brig. Gen. Elwood R. Quesada, chief, IX Fighter Command *(center)*.

up air activity and subsequent air support. Like a number of enthusiastic airmen, Gen. Hap Arnold (1-21) initially believed that air power alone could so crush Germany's military, economy, and morale that Overlord would be unnecessary. Later, however, this commander of the U.S. Army Air Force (USAAF) agreed that a land invasion would be required.

Ike's own air commanders were Maj. Gen. Lewis H. Brereton and Brig. Gen. Elwood R. ("Pete") Quesada (1-22). Unlike many senior Overlord officers who were veterans of World War I, Quesada was a mere thirty-seven years old. Brereton's IX Bomber Command provided softening-up effort—taking out bridges and so forth—before the invasion. The IX Troop Carrier Command provided transports that the Airborne units required, while the Ninth Air Force provided bombing support on D-Day itself.

As with Montgomery and Ramsay, Air Chief Marshal Sir Trafford Leigh-Mallory (1-23) reported directly to Ike. He was to assume control of the tactical operations of the strategic air forces after 1 June 1944. A tested fighter commander, he was inexperienced in strategic air defense, and Arnold, among others, doubted his suitability for this command.

1-23. British Air Marshal Sir Trafford Leigh-Mallory, commander in chief, Allied Expeditionary Air Forces.

1-24. Adolf Hitler, chancellor of the German *Reich* *(right)*, rides with Italian dictator Benito Mussolini *(left)* during their heyday.

The German commanders opposing the Allies were a curious mixture of real soldiers, well worthy of respect, and hacks whose only qualification for their positions was Chancellor Adolf Hitler's favor (1-24). In the early days of the war, Hitler's unorthodox tactics had often succeeded, but by the time of Overlord the German situation had so deteriorated that he was considerably more of a hindrance than a help to his *Wehrmacht* (armed forces).

Among Hitler's pets was Field Marshal Wilhelm Keitel (1-25), who, as chief of *Oberkommando der Wehrmacht* (OKW, or the Armed Forces High Command), was somewhat equivalent to the present chairman of the Joint Chiefs, had under him the Navy, *Luftwaffe* (Air Force), and Army high commands. Thus, Keitel was faced with an unusual situation: though Hitler was hardly Keitel's subordinate, Hitler was his chief of Army High Command. Ironically, Keitel was definitely a second-rate officer, and under normal circumstances he would have been lucky to attain field grade. Thanks to Hitler, however, he became a field marshal. From the *führer*'s point of view, Keitel's deficiencies were more

1-25. *Generalfeldmarschall* Wilhelm Keitel, chief of OKW *(left)*, chats with *Reichsführer*-SS Heinrich Himmler *(right)*, probably before the war.

1-26. *General der Artillerie* Alfred Jodl, chief of staff of the German Army. Hitler retained titular command.

than outweighed by his not being a Prussian, hence making him hostile to the Prussian power structure, and his absolute loyalty to Hitler.

At the time of Overlord, Heinrich Himmler, leader of the *Waffen-SS* (*Waffen–Schutz Staffel*, literally "Weapons Protection Squadron"), had reached the pinnacle of his power, and some considered him, rather than the popular Hermann Göring, as a possible successor to Hitler. Though the Waffen-SS divisions in Normandy and their parent organizations were under Himmler's leadership and were considered a military force of the *Reich*, they never attained the status of a fourth branch of the Wehrmacht. In battle, the Waffen-SS was subordinate to *Oberkommando des Heeres* (Army High Command), or Hitler.

Hitler's chief of staff was Col. Gen. Alfred Jodl (**1-26**). He was as brilliant as Keitel was mediocre, but just as devoted to Hitler's interests.

The top man in position to oppose the Allied landings was von Rundstedt (**1-27**), whose position was referred to as *Oberbefehlshaber West*, or OB West. Von Rundstedt was a sentimental favorite of the German Army and people, even though he was not a Nazi and had great contempt for Hitler. He left his post, ostensibly for "ill health," late in June. Actually, when Keitel had asked him, "What shall we do?" Rundstedt had snapped back, "Make peace, you fools. What else can you do?" Three days later he was out as OB West— but not for long. In September, Hitler restored him.

During von Rundstedt's absence, Field Marshal Günther von Kluge (**1-28**) took over OB West. His early optimism quickly dissipated after he assumed command. He became so convinced of the hopelessness of Germany's situation that he got word to anti-Hitler conspirators that, once convinced Hitler was dead, he would support a putsch.

1-27. Generalfeldmarschall Gerd von Rundstedt, commander in chief in the West. This photo was taken following his capture in 1945.

1-28. Generalfeldmarschall Günther von Kluge, successor to von Rundstedt as OB West. He is shown here with Hitler during the 1935 Fall Maneuvers.

1-29. Generalfeldmarschall Erwin Rommel, commander, Army Group B in Normandy.

Probably the best known of Hitler's generals in the West was Rommel (**1-29**). A man of much charm, he was a popular favorite despite his loss to Monty at Alamein. Even Rommel's opponents respected him as a gifted soldier and as a man of honor. In June 1944, his situation was far from enviable. Rommel's command included the armed forces in the Netherlands, the Fifteenth Army (which lay between Paris and Pas-de-Calais), and the Seventh Army in the Normandy area proper. He could also expect cooperation and a certain amount of tactical control over the 2d Parachute Corps. His reserves for Army Group B included the 2d, 116th, and 21st Panzer divisions, which lay some distance behind the Norman coast. These reserves, however, also came under the influence of *General der Panzertruppen* Leo Freiherr Geyr von Schweppenburg, chief of staff, Panzer Group West. Other available reserves (OKW Reserve, namely, 1st Panzer Group Corps under SS Gen. Sepp Dietrich and the Panzer *Lehr* [instructional] Division) could

1-30. *Generaloberst* Heinz Guderian, inspector general of Panzers.

be released only with the express permission of Keitel and Hitler. Thus, a highly fluid situation might find the Germans paralyzed and the frontline commanders—von Rundstedt and Rommel—unable to commit the best forces in the area to action.

Another well-known German general was Heinz Guderian (1-30). He was Hitler's armor tactician; after enjoying victories on the Eastern Front, his name was practically synonymous with tank warfare. No doubt Hitler depended upon Guderian to repeat his exploits in the West. But the situation in the West was quite different: the confines of the *bocage*, or hedgerows, made it difficult, if not impossible, to deploy a Panzer division "steppe-style" as in Russia. Hedgerows made it difficult to attack.

Col. Gen. Friedrich Dollman's Seventh Army would bear the brunt of the American attack during Overlord. Dollman (1-31) would commit suicide late in June and be succeeded by Gen. Paul Hausser (1-32). The first SS officer to command a Wehrmacht army, Hausser soon infiltrated its ranks with SS noncommissioned officers (NCOs).

Under the Seventh Army was the LXXXIV Corps commanded by Gen. Erich Marcks. As a colonel, Marcks (1-33) had been a public relations officer. In the early days of Nazism, he had been one of those who tried unsuccessfully to persuade President von Hindenburg to appoint Hitler chancellor of Germany. Marcks had lost a leg in Russia. Oddly enough, his birthday was 6 June.

1-31. Generaloberst Friedrich Dollman, commanding general, Seventh Army. Note on the right breast of Dollman's tunic the thread loops used to secure decorations and ribbon bars.

1-32. *Obergruppenführer* Paul Hausser, successor to Dollman as commander, Seventh Army, following Normandy. His rank was equivalent to generaloberst.

1-33. General der Artillerie Erich Marcks (*left*), commander of the Seventh Army's LXXXIV Corps, which lay within the Normandy sector.

1-34. *Reichsmarschall* Hermann Göring, chief of OKL (Luftwaffe High Command).

1-35. Gen. Adolf Galland, commander, German Fighter Command.

1-36. *Grossadmiral* Karl Dönitz, admiral of the fleet, *Kriegsmarine* (German Navy) and KM (Naval High Command).

Germany's Air Force High Command (*Oberkommando der Luftwaffe*, OKL) had the dubious distinction of being under the command of Hermann Göring (**1-34**), one of Hitler's oldest and most trusted henchmen. He had done well as a flier in World War I, and despite his unsavory character, "*unser* (our) *Hermann*" was a great popular favorite with the German people. Upon the Luftwaffe's maintaining some semblance of control over the airspace in northern Europe would depend Rommel's ability to move up quickly with his armored reserves. However, by the spring of 1944, the Allies' relentless bombing campaigns had left the Luftwaffe in a state of hopeless numerical inferiority and in poor shape to intervene against the Allied onslaught that was to come.

Göring's fighter commander was Gen. Adolf Galland (**1-35**). One of Germany's ace airmen, Galland was seriously handicapped by two circumstances. First, after the USAAF's heavy bombing raids deep into the German homeland, the Luftwaffe transferred much of its fighter strength from the French coast to the Home Defense units. Thus, many of the available fighters Galland could have used to repel or fend off an invasion lay at airfields deep in the Reich. Sec-ond, most of the advanced airfields he had planned to use had been so heavily bombed that he was forced to improvise landing areas.

To challenge seriously an invasion such as Overlord would have required a large surface Navy, which Germany no longer had. The two largest capital ships available to the chief of the Naval High Command (*Oberkommando der Marine*, OKM), Adm. Karl Dönitz (**1-36**)—*Tirpitz* and *Scharnhorst*—lay in port badly damaged. Thus, Dönitz had only two pocket battleships, two heavy cruisers, and four light cruisers (most of them in far-away ports) to face the enormous armada ready to cross the Channel. Dönitz was destined to succeed Hitler as führer of the German state.

The only ace in the hole for the *Kriegsmarine* (German Navy) was its relatively large number of smaller vessels, including five destroyers, about ten torpedo boats, and fifty to sixty E-boats, which lay about the ports of Normandy under Vice Adm. Theodor Krancke (**1-37**). Krancke also commanded various naval units ashore and the Navy's coastal batteries.

1-37. Adm. Theodor Krancke, chief of Naval Group West *(right)* speaks with Luftwaffe Gen. Johannes Jeschonneck.

CHAPTER 2 | Men and Machines

2-1. *Generalleutnant* Günther Blumentritt, OB West chief of staff to von Rundstedt.

AXIS

The German forces defending the beaches of Normandy comprised the LXXXIV Corps of Hitler's Seventh Army. Certainly, the LXXXIV Corps was not Hitler's "front line." Interviews with the German High Command after the war, in fact, indicated that by 1944 most of these units were of lower caliber than those on the Eastern Front.

This decline in quality occurred as the war strained Germany's capacity to provide fresh divisions to the Eastern Front meat grinder. Maj. Gen. Günther Blumentritt (2-1), chief of staff of OB West, remarked that, up to 1943, approximately sixty good divisions had been stationed in France but that these first-line units were withdrawn, replaced by battered units from the East in need of rest and reorganization. The continual shuffling of units in and out of France wreaked havoc with the local commanders' defensive planning. In the event of an Allied invasion, they would have only the exhausted, recuperating units available to hurl the invaders back. Hence, they created the concept of static (*bodenständige*) coastal divisions, each with the task of defending a designated tract of heavily fortified beachfront real estate (2-2).

Blumentritt recognized certain advantages of such a system. Static units could develop a detailed, specialized knowledge of and defense plans for their particular sector, while freeing the better-quality divisions for action in the East. The system likewise made efficient use of the material resources at hand, which were becoming scarcer with each passing month. Naturally, this system also had several drawbacks. The stationary divisions were just that—stationary—with little motor transport; these units were virtually locked into their respective sectors. Next, the very nature of the coastal division scheme seemed to promote an inflexible defense at best, leaving upper-level commanders limited options in case of situations requiring rapid deployment of forces. Finally, the comparatively meager field organization of these units was also unsatisfactory. They were in no sense full divisions capable of effectively taking the field, even assuming motor transport was available. Most divisions had

2-2. A German reinforced concrete observation post at Cherbourg. Note the camouflage paint scheme.

2-3. A tired German *unteroffizier,* or sergeant, comes on board battleship USS *Texas* on 7 June 1944.

only two infantry regiments and three artillery battalions, almost all of which were horse-drawn.

Inevitably, other personnel problems surfaced. Combatants in the stationary units, for example, tended to be considerably older than in the frontline divisions marching off to the Eastern Front. In 1944, the average age of the German soldier was 31.5 years, a full 6 years older than his American counterpart. Even though the 709th Division in Normandy did have young members, the average age in the division was 36. The fact that Hitler's Reich was scraping the bottom of its manpower barrel clearly showed in the faces of an Army now approaching middle-age (2-3).

2-4. Two Polish prisoners, likely *Volksdeutsche*, being interrogated on 15 June 1944.

2-5. Ten glum Mongolian *Freiwilligen* stand under guard on board a U.S. warship in the aftermath of the Normandy invasion.

In addition, few of the top-notch younger recruits and volunteers were posted to the stationary divisions. Germany's best and brightest men—of whom tens of thousands now lay buried on the steppes of the Soviet Union—were certainly underrepresented on the French coast. Indeed, recruiters steered many of the best, most highly motivated of Germany's youth away from the Army altogether, channeling them into Waffen-SS divisions and the Luftwaffe's elite *Fallschirmjäger* (paratrooper) regiments. This trend, over the long term, seemed to have had a somewhat chilling effect on the Army's morale. Though no one doubted the patriotism of the men in the coastal divisions, they lacked the vitality of their younger comrades.

Finally, while we cannot measure the physical fitness of the average German soldier in Normandy, we must recall that the Wehrmacht had considerably relaxed the physical standards of its entrance requirements. Thus, the coastal divisions acquired many individuals who ordinarily might have been considered unfit, such as those suffering from third-degree frostbite. For instance, one whole division in Normandy was composed entirely of men with stomach ailments.

Another trend that manifested itself during the middle war years also indicated that Germany had already worked through its manpower reserves. In June 1941, on the eve of its invasion of the Soviet Union, the German Army took great pride in its racial purity. Soon, however, the Eastern Front's drain on German manpower began to exact its toll, forcing the Wehrmacht to compromise its racial standards. It included *Volksdeutsche* (**2-4**), or "racial Germans," in the military and later accepted decidedly "non-Aryans" into the ranks of *Freiwillige* (volunteers) and *Hilfswillige* (auxiliaries).

2-6. American infantry round up civilian laborers and German and Italian soldiers on Omaha Beach during 6 June 1944. A wounded American at right stands on guard.

2-7. A 153mm field gun the Germans captured from the Russians and transported to the Normandy front.

By the late fall of 1941, Hitler authorized the enlistment of Russian prisoners of war (POWs) into labor battalions.

Ultimately, Russian combat battalions, or *Ost* (East) battalions, that were recruited in the fight against bolshevism went into action during the German offensive in the summer of 1943. When the offensive disintegrated, the Russian volunteers became so unreliable that, in September, OKW authorized transfer to the West of two Ost battalions for every German battalion. By May 1944, the Seventh Army included among its units twenty-three Ost battalions, or one-sixth of its total rifle battalions. In the Normandy sector, where the German LXXXIV Corps was stationed, eight of the forty-two battalions were filled with Russian recruits. Thus, forces confronting any Allied invasion attempt would hardly be the homogenous "Aryan" fighting force of June 1941 (**2-5**).

In addition to the coastal divisions defending Normandy's beaches, a multitude of miscellaneous hangers-on occupied the fortified French coast. These included a host of civilian laborers and *invalides* from the Italian Army (**2-6**), all employed in strengthening the Atlantic front against possible invasion.

If the overall quality of the troops along the French coast was suspect, so was the quality of their equipment. Much of the latest weaponry rolling off the beleaguered German assembly lines headed straight toward the Eastern Front. The equipment allotted to the coastal divisions consisted of either captured matériel or worn-out castoffs from frontline units. Prone to breakdowns and failures and plagued by parts' shortages, the aging equipment and weapons seriously hampered the effectiveness of the coastal divisions. The mix of captured French, Polish, Yugoslav, and Russian small arms and artillery (**2-7**) only served to ensure supply problems and confusion.

2-8. Generalleutnant Fritz Bayerlein *(right)*, commander, Panzer Lehr Division (here, an *oberstleutnant*) reports to General Cruewell during the heyday of the Afrika Korps.

2-9. A German infantry private (note the white piping on shoulder straps) demonstrates one of his prior occupations for his American captors on 15 June.

2-10. Karl-Wilhelm von Schlieben, commander, 709th Infantry Division. Shown here as an *oberst* early in the war.

As if the problems faced by the coastal divisions associated with supply, personnel, and logistics were not enough, France itself—totally apart from the formal Resistance movement—appeared to work a destructive influence on the combat effectiveness of the German troops stationed there for any length of time. Some German generals often thought of France as a vast convalescent center, where troops were sent to be "completely spoiled."

Fritz Bayerlein, commander of the Panzer Lehr Division (2-8), declared that over a period of years the overall condition, including combat readiness, of the infantry divisions stationed in France had progressively declined. In his postwar interview with the U.S. Army's Historical Division, he snorted acidly, "France is a dangerous country, with its wine, women, and pleasant climate. Troops who are there for any length of time become bad soldiers. They have done nothing but live well and send things home." He observed that units in the East just back from extended stays in France tended to "fail utterly" when under pressure; there seemed no reason to assume that they would perform differently in France itself. Bayerlein's painful condemnation of his own comrades in arms underscores yet another of the many problems faced by the German Seventh Army in France.

One of the mitigating circumstances Bayerlein ignored was the fact that, of necessity, many German troops in Normandy had to serve as construction laborers. Rommel had an ambitious construction and mine-laying program to fortify the French coastline that required vast numbers of laborers; however, the Fifteenth Army, which stood guard at Pas-de-Calais, received priority on both men and matériel. Not until January 1944 were three engineer battalions assigned to the LXXXIV Corps—two battalions for fortification construction and one for laying mines. Even when nearly an additional three thousand men from the French Labor Service pitched in, still more help was needed. As a result, the average German infantryman in Normandy found himself increasingly occupied with shoveling sand (2-9).

Typical of these improvised bands of "engineers" was the reserve battalion of the 709th Infantry Division, commanded by von Schlieben (2-10). Fully three days a week were reserved for construction work, with still more time devoted to transportation and guard duties. In view of the lack of the continuous training required for any unit, it was inevitable that the degree of combat readiness among the units in Normandy would deteriorate steadily. Alarmingly for the Germans, the 709th Division, manacled to its fortified positions along Utah Beach, was all too typical of the coastal divisions that would have to bear the brunt of the invasion force.

It would be misleading, however, to think that the coastal divisions were typical of the average German field division in 1944. The Wehrmacht's fully mobile, offensive divisions were still quite strong, well equipped, and in most cases at least adequately trained. In particular, the various Waffen-SS Panzer divisions, the Luftwaffe's Fallschirmjäger divisions, and the Army's Panzer Lehr divisions—all of which were available to the Germans during the Normandy invasion—were magnificent fighting machines.

Because almost the entire written records of the Seventh Army were lost in the chaos after the fall of Cherbourg, bringing the image of the average German soldier in Normandy into complete focus is not easy. However, at least in retrospect, German commanders did not seem to think much of the quality of the static divisions ensconced on the French coast. After the war, various divisional commanders and officers of the German High Command were cooperative with the Army's Historical Division and spoke freely of their shortcomings. A vanquished enemy's proclivity to search for excuses, however, dictates that the interviews be used with caution. The eminent American naval historian, Samuel Eliot Morison, cast a jaundiced eye on the postwar interviews of the German High Command, scornfully referring to the series as "alibi essays."

Without question, however, even aside from considerations of personnel quality, the average Wehrmacht infantry division of 1944 was far below standards that prevailed during the initial years of the war. Between 1938 and 1943, a German infantry division had nine rifle battalions apportioned to three regiments. A regiment's complement of twelve rifle and heavy weapons companies was rounded out by an infantry howitzer company and a company of antitank specialists. Each division also had two additional antitank and reconnaissance battalions. Incorporating a regiment of artillery, which consisted of one medium and three light battalions, brought the numbers of a typical German division to about 17,200 men, considerably stronger than its typical American counterpart.

In October 1943, Germany's dwindling manpower supply forced the Wehrmacht to initiate a drastic overhaul of its division structure. Each regiment had its number of battalions cut from three to two, reducing the new-style divisions to 13,656 effectives. No sooner was the ink dry on the organization charts when, in January 1944, Hitler mandated that divisional strength be reduced to 11,000 without affecting combat strength. Supply troops and other "overhead" were

Comparative Firepower of U.S. and German Infantry Divisions (1944)

	U.S.	German
Manpower strength (officers and enlisted)	14,037	12,769
Rifles/carbines	11,507	9,069
Pistols	1,228	1,981
Submachine guns	295	1,503
Light machine guns and automatic rifles	539	566
Heavy machine guns	90	90
60mm mortars	90	—
81mm mortars	54	48
120mm mortars	—	28
Bazookas	558[a]	108[b]
Flamethrowers	—	20
.50-caliber machine guns (U.S.); 20mm antiaircraft guns (German)	237	12
37mm antitank (AT) guns	13	—
57mm AT guns	57	—
75mm AT guns	—	35
75mm infantry howitzers	—	18
105mm howitzers	54[c]	36
155mm (U.S.)/150mm (German) howitzers	12	18[d]

a. Also 2,131 rifle grenade launchers
b. Either bazookas or AT rifles
c. 18 in cannon companies of infantry regiments
d. 6 were infantry howitzers, 2 in an infantry howitzer company assigned to each infantry regiment; each howitzer company also had 6 75mm howitzers.

2-12. Comparative firepower of U.S. and German infantry divisions in 1944.

eliminated, cutting total strength to 12,769, closer to Hitler's wishes (2-11). At company level, Hitler's mandate pared available personnel down to 140 enlisted men and 2 officers, compared to a U.S. standard of 183 men and 6 officers. However, these reductions tended to be offset by the German practice of increasing the number of automatic weapons. Thus, while the German division of 1944 numbered some 1,200 fewer troops than its American counterpart, it still possessed greater total firepower and a marked superiority in machine guns (2-12).

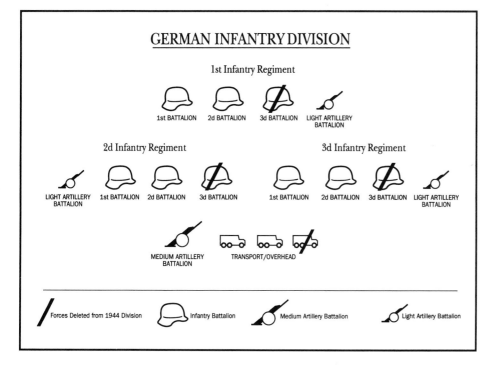

GERMAN INFANTRY DIVISION

1st Infantry Regiment

1st BATTALION 2d BATTALION 3d BATTALION LIGHT ARTILLERY BATTALION

2d Infantry Regiment

LIGHT ARTILLERY BATTALION 1st BATTALION 2d BATTALION 3d BATTALION

3d Infantry Regiment

1st BATTALION 2d BATTALION 3d BATTALION LIGHT ARTILLERY BATTALION

MEDIUM ARTILLERY BATTALION TRANSPORT/OVERHEAD

Forces Deleted from 1944 Division Infantry Battalion Medium Artillery Battalion Light Artillery Battalion

2-11. Comparison of 1943 and 1944 German infantry divisions.

91st Infantry (Air Landing) Division

In the vicinity of the prospective American landing areas, there were only a few attack grade divisions (2-13) that could hope to intervene. One of these was the 91st Infantry Division, commanded by Maj. Gen. Wilhelm Falley (2-14). The 91st comprised much of the offensive punch for LXXXIV Corps; accordingly, Falley's primary mission was to repel any Allied airborne landings. Since the Germans anticipated that any Allied attack might well descend on France's seaports, the division was posted near Cherbourg, with Falley's headquarters located in Picauville. While the division possessed only two regular infantry regiments—the 1057th and 1058th—it boasted three full battalions of artillery.

In May 1944, the 91st Division received reinforcements—the 6th Fallschirmjäger Regiment. Its commander, Baron von der Heydte (2-15), established his command post just north of the village of Périers. When its parent unit, the 2d Fallschirmjäger Division, was sent East in November 1943, the regiment had stayed behind in Germany to provide a core with which to form a third division of paratroopers.

Von der Heydte's elite regiment was composed of youngsters whose average age was 17.5 years; however, the unit was well trained and well armed. To a man, the regiment had conducted nine training jumps—three of those at night. Moreover, the regiment was at full strength, with 3,457 men under arms, including three battalions and a heavy weapons company of machine guns and mortars. Nor was the regiment short on leadership. Von der Heydte was a hero who had led the regiment's 1st Battalion in the bitter fighting on Crete in 1941. Clearly, the Fallschirmjägers would be a force to reckon with, and they augmented the offensive capability of the 91st Division to a significant degree.

Other reinforcements of a far less scintillating nature, namely the 100th Panzer Replacement Battalion, came to join the 91st Division. This battalion came equipped only with a handful of captured French and Russian light tanks, hence the unit was of comparatively little value.

So, with units and personnel ranging from elite to poor, the 91st Division stood ready to repel any invasion attempt from across the Channel. The generally high quality of this division would ensure that any Allied move inland from the beach would come at a great cost.

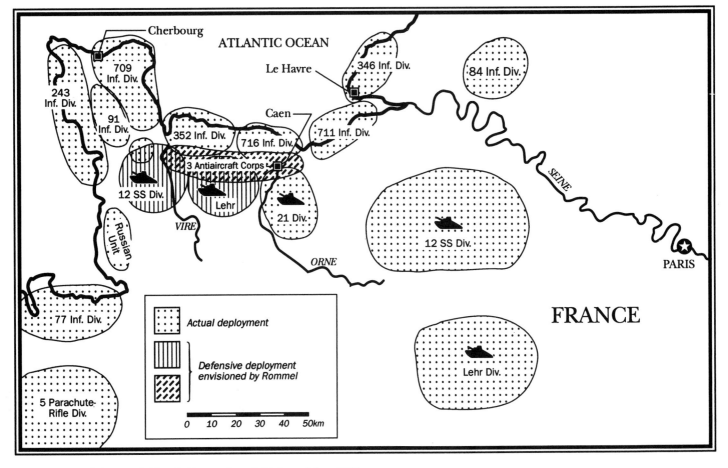

2-13. Positions of German divisions in Normandy and vicinity on 6 June 1944.

2-14. *Generalmajor* Wilhelm Falley, commander, 91st Infantry Division *(right center)*, confers with General der Artillerie Erich Marcks of the LXXXIV Corps.

2-15. Oberst Baron Friedrich-August Freiherr von der Heydte, commander, 6th Fallschirmjäger Regiment. Shown here as a major, listening to a radio in his command car.

352d Infantry Division

Resting in the defensive positions along Omaha Beach from the Vire Estuary to Port-en-Bessin-Huppain was a full attack division—namely, the 352d Infantry, commanded by Gen. Dietrich Kraiss (**2-16**). In several notable regards, the 352d differed somewhat from the coastal divisions. Unlike some of the other static units whose personnel were completely untested, the men in the 352d were skilled, combat-hardened veterans of the desperate fighting in the Soviet Union. Though formed as recently as November 1943, the division had at its core the remnants of the 268th and 321st Infantry divisions, which earlier in the year had been withdrawn from Army Group Center in the East.

Additionally, rather than having two regiments as 1944 standards prescribed, the 352d had a full complement of nine rifle battalions organized into three regiments. Deployed along the coast were the 726th Grenadier Regiment, under *Oberst* Korfes, and the 916th Grenadier Regiment, under *Oberst* Ernst Goth. These two units lay entrenched in eight concrete bunkers that contained guns of 75mm or greater and in thirty-five pillboxes, six mortar pits, thirty-five rocket sites, and eighty-five machine gun nests.

Periodically, the division rotated units out of the sandy frontline fortifications into the respite of reserve status, well behind the beaches. On the morning of 6 June, Major Meyer's 915th Grenadier Regiment filled that reserve role, having been billeted in the town of Bayeux since 20 May.

The 352d enjoyed a particular advantage over the other Wehrmacht divisions in Normandy, thanks to good

2-16. Generalleutnant Dietrich Kraiss, commander, 352d Infantry Division. Kraiss wears a WWI-period Iron Cross 1st Class, with a "W" for Kaiser "Wilhelm" rather than a swastika in the center.

hunting. In May the Germans shot down a carrier pigeon, whose message for the Allies suggested that elements of the 352d were posted in the coastal fortifications. So the Americans, unaware of the presence of a full attack division, planned on meeting only a solitary regiment of an over-extended coastal division on Omaha Beach. Ironically, of all the sectors along the Normandy coast, Omaha Beach was the only area where Rommel possibly had sufficient troops to throw an invasion attempt into the sea.

SPECIFIC WEAPONS

In many ways, the geography of northern France was one of the premier weapons in the German arsenal. At Omaha Beach in particular the terrain was relatively easy to defend, even with simply rifle fire and grenades. The following profile of Omaha Beach provides critical yet obvious clues to understanding the difficulties the U.S. V Corps faced on the morning of 6 June.

Splashing ashore during low tide, the invading troops would have to traverse nearly 300 yards of a flat, wet beach covered with obstacles and mines. After reaching a band of dry sand constituting a high tide marker, the Americans would have to scale a concrete seawall that, on its seaward side, was faced with a narrow bank of large, smooth pebbles. Crunching forward past the seawall, the infantrymen would become ensnared in a ruffle of concertina wire. A flat, grassy plain, ranging from 150 to 300 yards in width, would next greet the invaders and offer nothing in the way of cover. At this point the terrain rose up from the beach in a series of steep bluffs, insurmountable even by tracked vehicles. Passage to the interior could be made only by way of several deep, eroded ravines that gouged their way into the French countryside beyond. Narrow dirt roads slithered through these ravines, or "draws" as the Americans called them, and connected the beach area with a main road that paralleled the shore, roughly one kilometer in the rear.

After viewing Omaha Beach from the Americans' pre-invasion perspective, one plainly sees how the Wehrmacht's static coastal defense divisions expected to make it rough going for any would-be invader. Note, for example, the high bluffs to the right and left and the "draw" at the center illustrated in photo **2-17**. From their positions high atop the bluffs overlooking the beach (**2-18**), the soldiers of the 352d Division enjoyed a superb field of fire that enabled them to fire *into* the incoming American landing craft.

Other obstacles, natural and manmade, challenged the invaders (**2-19**). Photo **2-20** shows vividly how the ever-changing weather along the Norman coast could play into the Germans' hands. And even after the Allies had passed

2-17. The approach to Omaha Beach as seen from the PT boat that carried Adm. Harold R. Stark ashore on an inspection tour of the Allied beachhead on 14 June 1944.

2-18. View from a German 75mm PAK43 gun position in a Normandy pillbox. PAK stands for *Panzerabwehrkanone* (antitank gun).

2-19. Cliffs of Normandy at high tide and beach obstacles in the surf.

2-20. View of an invasion beach.

the beaches, they would face the formidable hedgerows (2-21). These centuries-old boundaries converted every small field into a fortress.

A number of German measures, however, were designed to stop the enemy before he could reach land. For example, the mines pictured in photo 2-22 were undoubtedly destined for the waters surrounding the Cotentin Peninsula. Before landing craft could approach the French coast, numerous sea lanes into the beaches had to be swept clear of these mines. Teller mines were usually planted several hundred feet out in the surf, where they would be covered with water at high tide, thus providing defense against landing craft (2-23 and 2-24).

Numerous gun emplacements on the beach stood ready to contest the landings (2-25). Once into the surf and onto

2-21. *Le bocage*—the hedgerows of Normandy.

2-22. Railway car full of mines abandoned by the Germans at Cherbourg. This photo was taken on 3 July 1944.

2-23. German Teller mines affixed to posts and planted in the surf west of Omaha near Pointe du Hoc.

2-24. Teller mine attached to a pole fashioned from a tree trunk on Utah Beach.

2-25. A 75mm L24 gun turret from a Mark IIIN Panzer in place on Omaha Beach provides evidence of the effort to recycle outdated armored equipment.

2-26. German machine-gun position at La Grande Vey between Utah and Omaha beaches.

2-27. German pillbox in use as an Army command post after the invasion. Note American equipment.

2-28. An incomplete German 105mm gun emplacement of reinforced concrete construction, two miles inland from Fort St.-Marcouf, north of Utah Beach.

the beaches, invading troops would draw small-arms fire (2-26). The gun trained on them from the pillbox (2-27) was possibly an 88mm PAK44. Photos **2-28** and **2-29** show German gun emplacements. Often the Germans were forced into less protected, impromptu, temporary defenses due to lack of time and matériel.

Once off the beaches, the Americans would have to traverse mine-infested areas such as that pictured in **2-30**.

2-29. A 50mm gun emplacement on the beach at La Grande Vey between Utah and Omaha beaches.

2-30. Leaving hurriedly, the Germans failed to remove this minefield sign.

2-31. Teller mines and other antipersonnel weapons lie on the beach at Normandy, after being "tamed" by Allied sappers.

2-32. The business end of a German bomb hangs suspended from a cliff overlooking Omaha Beach. The precise location is not known, but likely it was Pointe du Hoc, where the 2d Ranger Battalion landed.

2-33. German flamethrower near Fort de Foucarville, inland from Utah Beach.

The task of securing the beachhead thus included clearing all mines and obstacles (2-31). Other Nazi weapons included bombs (2-32), flamethrowers (2-33), and a curious device called a "Beetle" (2-34). Powered by two electric motors and stuffed with explosives, these weapons were used as mobile antilanding-craft mines.

Less exotic was the 88mm Flak 42 gun (2-35). One of the most feared of all German weapons, it possessed great

2-34. German remote-control "Beetle" miniature tank photographed shortly after the initial landings. Note the socks drying in the background.

2-35. German 88mm Flak 42 gun. This example was photographed in Sicily, 7 August 1943.

2-36. German tank, or panzer, PzKpfw *(Panzerkampfwagen)* IV Aus H with 75mm L48 gun. This example taken near Sezze, Italy, on 29 May 1944.

2-37. German *Kettenkraftrad,* or tracked motorcycle, captured in Normandy. This photo was taken on 14 June 1944 near Isibny. An American soldier sits astride while other soldiers repair the unit for their own transportation.

2-38. German MG-42 machine gun.

range, accuracy, and penetrating power. Equally formidable was the PzKpfw (*Panzerkampfwagen*) IV Aus H (**2-36**). This was probably the most numerous German tank type in Normandy. German armor did not get into the fight against the Americans until relatively late, after the beachhead was secured, which was fortunate for the Americans. Had Rommel's reserve and the OKW reserves been able to penetrate quickly toward the beaches, Bradley's First Army would have encountered considerably tougher resistance.

To provide some measure of mobility to their troops, the Germans used large numbers of vehicles such as the tracked motorcycle (**2-37**). Mobility, however, was sadly lacking in the coastal divisions.

2-39. Czech Brno light machine gun, captured and put to use by the Germans.

The MG-42 machine gun (**2-38**) was a much-feared weapon and was first used in North Africa in 1942. It had an astonishingly high rate of fire (1,200 rounds per minute [rpm]), excellent portability, and interchangeable barrels that could be switched out in five seconds. It was recommended that barrels be changed every 250 rounds. The Germans were also not above utilizing captured weapons (**2-39**) despite the problems with spare parts and ammunition supply that arose when a large number and variety of captured weapons were used.

The Walther pistol (**2-40**) was the standard German side arm—useless at long range but well suited for the close fighting in Normandy's houses and hedgerows. Apart from a German helmet, it was one of the most highly prized souvenirs of the ETO. The MP-40 was the Wehrmacht's standard submachine gun and was practically the badge of the German Army.

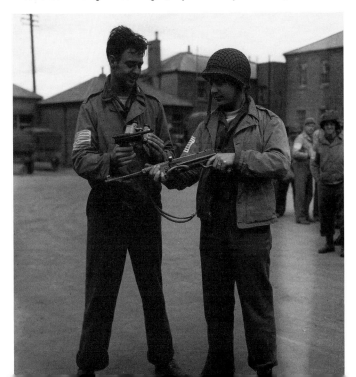

2-40. American troops in England examine two captured German weapons—a Walther P-38 9mm pistol and an MP-40 machine pistol.

2-41. Captured German rifles, bazooka, and range finder.

2-42. German *Panzerfäuste* (armored fists)—crude, one-shot bazookas, rigged for demolition toward the end of the war. Note stencil reading *"Vorsicht! Starker Feuerstrahl!"* ("Caution! Strong flame jet!")

Photo 2-41 shows a variety of German weapons, once again illustrating Germany's supply problems and the relatively low priority given to the Normandy defenses. We cannot identify either the top or bottom rifles pictured; the Germans may have captured them. The second rifle from the top is a *Gewehr* 41 automatic rifle. Very heavy, weighing 11 pounds, this rifle was usually the first weapon to be discarded. Of several thousand made, most were sent to the East and lost.

The second rifle from the bottom is a Karabiner 98K Mauser rifle, the standard infantry weapon during World War II. It remained in production through 1945 since development of automatic rifles never reached the point where bolt-action production could be eliminated. Still, rather than sending machine guns and machine pistols to the old boys in France, their superiors gave them Mausers.

The bazooka is an 8.8cm *Raketen Panzerbüchse* 54 (rocket tank-cylinder) *Panzerschreck* (tank terror). The Germans developed it from captured U.S. M-1 2.36-inch rocket launchers. It was first issued to troops on the Eastern Front in 1943. The face shield, which incorporated the rear sight, is missing from this example.

The *Panzerfäuste*, or armored fists (2-42), enjoyed wide use on both fronts, particularly later in the war. The advent of heavy Soviet armor in 1943 increased the Wehrmacht's demand for a light but powerful antitank weapon for infantry. The first version appeared in late 1941. The Model 50 (visible at left) likely saw some use in Normandy, while the Model 100 (visible at right) did not go into production until November 1944.

This weapon consisted of a steel tube with a sight and trigger mechanism on top (visible in example at bottom). A rocket-propelled bomb, fitted with a hollow head charge and flexible fins, was placed in and fired from the forward end of the tube, which was then discarded. Hauptmann (Capt.) Eduard Schatz, a former German officer who had served on the Eastern Front and is now deceased, summed up the *Panzerfäuste* for Mr. Wenger: "Cheap, effective, inaccurate except at close range, and suicidal to operate."

MEN AND MACHINES

Allied

The Allies' initial objectives were to transport the troops across the English Channel as swiftly and safely as possible and to land them on the designated beaches with a minimum of casualties. This task, code-named Neptune, was assigned to the Allied navies.

For covering firepower, the U.S. Navy had three of its four oldest battleships at Normandy; the only one not present was *New York* (BB-34). *Nevada* (2-43) was the only battleship in the Force "U" Bombardment Group. It had been completely rebuilt after the severe damage it sustained in the Pearl Harbor raid: the mainmast aft was cut down and the forward superstructure rebuilt and fitted with a modern antiaircraft (AA) battery. The main armament was ten 14-inch guns in four turrets. *Nevada* still retained its complement of OS2U Kingfisher observation planes.

2-43. Battleship *Nevada* (BB-36) in 1944.

Two battleships served in the Force "O" Bombardment Group. *Texas* (**2-44**), which had rendered illustrious service in WWI, had the same main armament as *Nevada*, but in five turrets. Now moored near Houston, *Texas* remains the only surviving capital ship from its generation. *Arkansas* (**2-45**) was the helpmate for *Texas* in the Force "O" Bombardment Group. Unique among American battleships, *Arkansas* was the sole survivor from the 12-inch gun class. Its main armament was twelve 12-inch guns in six turrets.

One of the many *Gleaves* (*Benson*)-class destroyers of the Western Naval Task Force was *Thompson* (**2-46**), which participated in the Force "O" Bombardment Group with *Texas* and *Arkansas*.

Landing Craft and Ships

How and where to procure enough landing craft for Overlord without seriously shortchanging other theaters of operation were difficult, ongoing problems throughout its planning stages and well into the spring of 1944. To illustrate the vast diversity of craft needed to invade the continent successfully, we will discuss selected types of landing craft and ships. Not all of these craft were used specifically to land troops and equipment; each had specialized functions in Neptune.

Landing *ships* were commissioned vessels and kept deck logs similar to any other combatant vessel. The landing *craft*, however, kept no such records; therefore, determining exactly when and where a particular photo was taken is sometimes questionable.

The LCI(L)—landing craft, infantry (stores carrier) (**2-47**)—was a 160-foot-long, diesel-powered, personnel-carrying craft. It could carry two hundred fully equipped men, seated, and could disembark from two ramps in 5 minutes. The LCI(L)'s speed was 12.5 knots.

2-44. Battleship *Texas* (BB-35) on 1 April 1944.

2-45. Battleship *Arkansas* (BB-33) shown here on 23 September 1942.

2-46. Destroyer *Thompson* (DD-627) seen from *Arkansas* during preparations for Normandy, late May 1944.

2-47. An LCM makes fast alongside *LCI(L)-95* off Utah Beach, 12 June 1944.

2-48. *LCF-22* stands offshore during the invasion rehearsals at Slapton Sands, off the coast of Great Britain.

2-49. An LCM, *PA13-2,* stands ready to take a jeep on board from a Coast Guard–manned transport during June 1944.

The LCF—landing craft, flak (**2-48**)—was a converted LCT (landing craft, tank) that provided E-boat protection, AA cover, and protection for the landing parties in its close support role. This was actually a British ship with an American crew—a curious form of reverse lend-lease.

The LCM—landing craft, mechanized (**2-49**), 50 feet long—was a general purpose, diesel-powered, shipborne landing craft designed specifically for ship-to-shore ferry service. It was capable of landing a 30-ton tank, other motor vehicles, or sixty men, but it could not be lowered while loaded. The LCM's speed was a rip-roaring six knots. This particular LCM is from APA-13, USS *Joseph T. Dickman*.

The LCT—landing craft, tank (**2-50**)—was a larger vessel capable of landing up to fifty-five men and eleven vehicles. Its length averaged 190 feet, with a speed of six knots. There seems to be no rigid conformance to what the various landing craft were designed to carry. Here the LCT (**2-51**) carries troops rather than vehicles ashore.

2-50. *LCT-520* releasing its load of trucks on 11 June 1944. Note how shallow the water is— barely up to the thighs of the crews near the vessel.

2-51. British *LCT-2008*, operating under the American flag, approaches the invasion beaches on 7 June.

2-52. British *LCT(R)-48* turns away from the Normandy beaches after delivering its rockets.

2-53. An LCVP, *PA30-31*, pulls away from its mother ship during pre-invasion loading operations.

2-54. *LST-325* and *LST-388* unload at low tide during the resupply operations of 12 June. Note the barrage balloons, single 40mm AA guns, and "Danforth"-style kedge anchor.

The LCT(R)—landing craft, tank (rocket) (2-52)—is, once again, a British vessel operating under the American flag. Many LCTs were converted to quite specialized uses, in this case as a platform for launching 5-inch rockets.

The LCVP—landing craft, vehicle, personnel—was a small, ramped, shipborne craft designed to carry one vehicle, or up to thirty-six men, as the photo indicates (2-53). The LCVP was the "standard" small landing craft. This particular one came from *Thomas Jefferson* (APA-30), craft number 31.

The LSTs—landing ships, tank (2-54)—were commissioned ships proper, with much larger capacities than the landing craft. They could carry three hundred troops and sixty vehicles. Notwithstanding their large size these ships had an extremely shallow draft. Their speed was nine knots.

The DUKW—truck, amphibious, 2.5 tons, 6x6 (2-55)—was a general purpose, gasoline-powered amphibious vehicle. The term did not originate with the Navy but stemmed from the manufacturer's code: *D* = 1942, *U* = utility, *K* = front-wheel drive, *W* = two rear-drive axles. The designation was inevitably corrupted to "Duck." It could travel up to 50 miles per hour (mph) on land and 6.5 mph in the water.

Just a few weeks before D-Day, Admiral King sent sixty U.S. Coast Guard cutters (2-56) to a U.S. naval base in England to be converted to rescue ships. They stood by off both the American and British landing beaches to pick up survivors from sunken or damaged vessels.

2-55. The Army DUKW "Jesse James" trudges through the surf to land its load of supplies on 11 June.

2-56. Two U.S. Coast Guard 83-foot patrol boats operate as rescue craft off the Normandy beaches.

The Rhino ferry (2-57 and 2-58) was a 42-foot-by-176-foot outboard-powered pontoon barge. Rhinos carried matériel from transports and LSTs to the beaches, when the beach shelving was too gradual to allow a closer approach by the larger vessels. Rhinos had deck space for thirty to forty vehicles.

2-57. A Rhino ferry is linked with *LST-322* and takes on a full cargo of invasion vehicles during pre-invasion exercises off the English coast.

2-58. A Rhino ferry loaded with personnel and vehicles and a barrage balloon flies overhead.

Aircraft and Other Equipment

Allied air power helped prepare for Overlord by heavily bombing German industries deep in the Fatherland and disrupting the rail systems leading to strategic points in Normandy. Aircraft, of course, dropped Airborne units prior to and provided cover for the actual landings.

Fighters included two particularly well-beloved types. Though the P-51 Mustang had made its entry to the war some months before, the Thunderbolt (2-59) was still the workhorse of the USAAF fighter arm. It was so incredibly rugged that some pilots did not want to fly the P-51 (2-60). The latter, however, soon proved itself. It possessed maneuverability comparable to that of the British Spitfire, superior speed, and the unsurpassed range needed to accompany the Eighth Air Force's heavy bombers all the way to their targets and back to England. More than any other aircraft it was responsible for clearing the skies over France in advance of D-Day.

2-59. Republic P-47 Thunderbolt.

2-60. North American P-51 Mustang, the nemesis of the Luftwaffe day fighter pilot.

2-61. Martin B-26 Marauder.

2-62. Douglas A-20 Havoc.

The B-26 and A-20 (**2-61** and **2-62**) were the backbone of the Ninth Air Force's medium and light bombardment force. They helped destroy bridges, thus tying up and rerouting military vehicle traffic before the invasion. The almost legendary, user-friendly B-17 heavy bomber (**2-63**) played quite a significant role in quelling the aerial opposition to the invasion. B-17 bombing raids deep into the German homeland tied down Luftwaffe fighter squadrons that otherwise might have been deployed closer to the Channel.

The mainstay of the USAAF transport commands was the C-47 (**2-64**). It saw extensive action with the IX Transport Command, airlifting the troops and supplies of the 82d and 101st Airborne divisions into Normandy throughout the campaign.

2-63. B-17F Flying Fortress. This example is the F variant, already being superseded in large numbers by the G model.

2-64. Douglas C-47.

Infantry alone would not be enough to hold onto the beaches. Heavy vehicles like the M-3 half-track (**2-65**) and armor such as the Sherman tank (**2-66** and **2-67**) were needed to provide the Army with the requisite strength and mobility to move inland. And who can recall World War II without bringing to mind the ubiquitous jeep (**2-68**)? Once in place, guns such as the M-7 (**2-69**) came into full play.

A triumph of GI ingenuity was the hedgerow "plow"

2-65. Army White M-3 half-track rolls onto causeway from the ramp of an LCT. The causeway is composed of Rhino barges. Note the gas can below and in front of the windshield. Navy personnel, identified by circular bands around the bottom of their helmets, direct the activity.

2-66. An M-4A2 Sherman tank from a French unit rolls out of an LST onto the sands of Utah Beach.

2-67. The American M-4 Sherman "Hurricane" with wading kit rolls onto Utah Beach during 6 June. The tank crews fully expected to have to come onto the beaches in several feet of water, hence they modified the air intakes with breather hoods to prevent water from being pulled into the engine. This particular vehicle has a strange mixture of U.S/British markings.

(2-70). Even tanks could not penetrate these incredibly dense growths until mid-July, when Sgt. Curtis Culin invented this plow out of angle iron. Mounted on a tank, it could slice through the obstacles that had been such a maddening problem.

In addition to confrontational combat, the Allies also depended upon Airborne troops. These men were so thoroughly equipped that it is a wonder that they were able to

2-68. Army jeep "Dam Yankee" is towed ashore after floundering in the surf on 12 June. Note the black driver and the censored vehicle unit data on the front bumper. Just like the tanks, this vehicle is also fitted with an amphibious breathing tube.

2-69. An Army M-7 Priest self-propelled, 106mm howitzer, "Big Chief," from Battery B, 42d Field Artillery, waits to go on board an LCT at Dartmouth, England, on 1 June 1944. Breather hoods are just visible in the rear, and a sign on its front says that the vehicle is supposed to load onto *LCT-234*. The sign in the background, "Simonds Ales, Wines, and Spirits," suggests that this building might be perhaps a haunt of American servicemen.

2-70. Hedgerow "plow" affixed to front of an M-5A1 Stuart light tank.

move at all, let alone swiftly. Though certainly geared toward the specialized requirements of a paratrooper, the equipment provided a parachutist rifleman (**2-71**) included many of the standard items carried by the average American infantryman, such as the M-1 Garand rifle with 8-round clip, cartridge belt with canteen, and hand grenades. Other items included a parachute and pack, antiflash headgear and gloves, pocket compass, machete, .45-caliber Colt automatic pistol, flares, and message book. The equipment of a rifle grenadier (**2-72**) was similar in some respects to that of a rifleman, except the rifle grenadier was equipped with a set

of binoculars and a 1903 Springfield rifle.

In addition to their equipment, each parachutist carried a small kit of emergency rations (**2-73**) that included:

4 pieces of chewing gum
2 bouillon cubes
2 Nescafé instant coffees, 2 sugar cubes, and creamers
4 Hershey bars
1 pack of Charms candy
1 package pipe tobacco
1 bottle of water purification tablets.

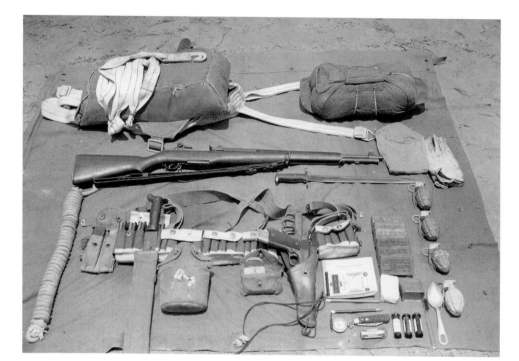

2-71. Equipment carried by a parachutist rifleman.

2-72. Parachutist equipment for a rifle grenadier.

American Infantry Divisions

Despite all the new weapons developed for amphibious warfare, on D-Day the mainstay of the U.S. assault would be the ordinary infantryman. During the first day of the invasion, three U.S. infantry divisions would land on the Normandy beaches.

The U.S. infantry division evolved from the WWI "square" division, which was composed of two brigades, and each brigade, in turn, was composed of two regiments. This organization was designed to concentrate the greatest mass of infantry in the shortest front possible and was admirably suited to sustained combat and the static trench warfare of World War I.

But developments in armor tactics and the changes brought about by the blitzkrieg tactics of the German Wehrmacht forced the armed forces of the world to rethink the makeup and role of an infantry division. American divisions went to a "triangulated" structure (which they retain to this day), where only three rifle regiments were used—one regiment would "fix" the enemy; a second would move against him, while a third lay in reserve. This restructuring enabled the modern divisions to be more flexible and to adapt to more fluid circumstances, so uncharacteristic of World War I.

The advent of hostilities was required, however, to wrest the U.S. Army from the grip of inertia. When the United States declared war in December 1941, American infantry divisions still retained the old "square" structure, even though the field testing had been completed and recommendations made far in advance for the triangular division.

Ironically, on 6 June, because the U.S. 1st Infantry Division was to execute a frontal assault on Omaha Beach (which would require a "critical mass" in infantry), the division reverted temporarily to a "squared" organization of four infantry regiments, with elements of the 29th Infantry Division attached until 7 June.

2-73. Emergency parachute rations.

CHAPTER 3

Rehearsal, Training, and Preparation

The period leading up to Overlord was exceedingly busy, suspenseful, and fraught with the possibilities of disruption. The absorption into the British Isles of over 1.5 million foreign soldiers, sailors, and airmen was in itself a sociological problem. At least they spoke the same language, although many a bewildered GI struggling to understand a British regional accent might have disputed that. Occasional resentments arose, as exemplified by the Tommies' crack that the trouble with the Yanks was they were "overpaid, oversexed, and over here." The GI's riposte had a sting at the end: What bothered the British, they stated, was that they were "underpaid, undersexed, and under Eisenhower." A little less discipline on the part of the Americans, a little less forbearance on the part of the British, and the delicate web of British-

American cooperation would have been in need of constant reweaving. As it was, at the person-to-person level the situation worked well enough, but it would be useless to pretend that all was sweetness and light at the planning and command level. Such serious differences existed between the British and Americans in objectives and methodology that it is a genuine tribute to all concerned that they were able to formulate a joint strategy and act upon it.

Although Americans were sited as far north as Rosneath, Scotland, most of the action centered around the Channel ports. Because incoming U.S. troops landed in the western ports, for convenience they remained in that general locality while the British used the more easterly sites. The amount of time, effort, and training necessary to prepare for Overlord, so that every man would know precisely what he was supposed to do and be ready and able to do it, can well be imagined. Training exercises were under way as early as the autumn of 1943 (**3-1**).

Admiral Wilkes was responsible for material readiness of all landing craft taking part in Overlord and for the training of all personnel involved directly in the landing efforts. Characterized by Morison as "a bundle of nervous energy," Wilkes had problems crop up continually. For example, in April 1944, all landing craft had to undergo extensive alterations, requiring new radio equipment and door modifications.

Capt. Chauncey Camp commanded the Far Shore Service Group. This included the repair ship *Adonis* (ADL-4)—converted from *LST-83*—and a host of service craft, ferries, refueling trawlers, and rescue vessels.

Photos **3-2** through **3-5** give us glimpses of an early exercise held at Woolacombe* on 31 October 1943. Some time later, the Overlord planners discovered Slapton Sands,

---

* This name may be a contraction of the names of two villages, Wool and Coombe, in the vicinity of which American men were training in cliff climbing.

3-1. Rear Admiral Wilkes *(left)* **and Capt. Chauncey Camp** *(right)* watch a dawn landing exercise at Woolacombe, England, on 31 October 1943.

3-2. Landing craft swing out from shore, en route to Woolacombe for landing rehearsals during 31 October.

3-3. Crewmen in slickers and life vests bail frantically to clear water from a broached LCVP during the Woolacombe exercises.

3-4. Troops splash through the surf at Woolacombe as they disembark from an LCVP.

3-5. An Army staff sergeant and captain—both quite wet—watch impassively as the Woolacombe landings unfold. The captain totes an M-1 carbine, and the sergeant wears an inflatable life belt—standard equipment in the landing craft.

3-6. An American soldier reads a signboard erected at Slapton Sands on 29 December 1943 during the evacuation.

3-7. Street scene in Slapton Sands during the civilian evacuation.

IMPORTANT

PUBLIC MEETINGS
will be held as under

FRIDAY
Nov. 12th
11 a.m. EAST ALLING
2-30 p.m. STOKENHAM

Earl Fortescue, M.C., The Lord L
in the Chair.

SATURDAY
Nov. 13th
11 a.m. BLACKAWTON CH
2-30 p.m. SLAPTON VILLAGE

Sir John Daw, J.P., Chairman Devon County
in the Chair.

THE AREA AFFECTED

3-8. A young English girl during the evacuation.

a well-nigh perfect spot for such maneuvers. It was located somewhat to the south of Torquay, and its terrain—a fine red gravel beach backed by grassy slopes—closely resembled that of the Normandy beaches (3-5). The V Corps would use this area; unfortunately, that meant that the civilian inhabitants would have to be evacuated to allow Overlord training and rehearsals (3-6). This evacuation took place in late December 1943. In photo 3-7, a local woman smokes and a Bobby looks on while some of the new residents, an American V Corps sergeant and two buddies, chat. The young girl pictured in photo 3-8 looks pensive. One can well believe that the inhabitants were less than thrilled to be removed from their homes.

Photo 3-9 shows the terrain of Slapton Sands. While

3-9. The broad beaches near Slapton Sands. Note the grassy slopes similar to those encountered in Normandy.

3-10. *LST-322* disgorges a portion of its cargo into a Rhino ferry off Slapton Sands.

3-11. Convoy of LCTs ply the waters off Slapton Beach, 10 January 1944.

training there was quite thorough, the constant arrivals of new equipment and green crews slowed down the pace and made the exercises more difficult (**3-10** and **3-11**).

Gradually the exercises increased in intensity and realism (**3-12**). During practice on 17 March 1944, what in normal times was a pleasant boardwalk running in front of beach cottages served as a background for landing craft lumbering in (**3-13**), with M-4 tanks already on the waterfront. Photo **3-14** shows a group of LCVPs heading for the beach.

3-12. Black soldiers roll off a Rhino ferry and land their jeep. The technician 5th grade at center is apparently attached directly to the First Army.

3-13. Landing practice on 17 March 1944.

3-14. *LCI-323* at left appears to be dead in the water, while the covey of LCVPs approaches the strand.

3-15. An L-4 Piper observation plane passes overhead after the LCVPs make their dash for the beach.

3-16. The landing takes place.

3-17. An infantryman's-eye view of the beach obstructions at Slapton Beach.

After they made their dash, an L-4 Piper observation plane surveys the situation (**3-15**). In a scene that would be reenacted thousands of times in the coming months, the landing is successfully completed (**3-16**). Sherman tanks with amphibious breathing hoods come ashore, flanked at right by *LCT-271*, which is unloading vehicles and personnel. The men on the beach are penetrating the barbed-wire barricades erected to simulate Normandy's beach obstacles.

Photo **3-17** shows a large group of infantrymen already past the barbed wire and proceeding up the slope behind the beach. One wonders what was going through their minds. "Surely the actual assault won't be that easy? What will the real beach be like? For that matter, would we ever face the Normandy beaches? Perhaps the whole invasion would be canceled." Anything was possible in war.

These maneuvers were under constant observation both from those who were essentially part of the team (**3-18**) to the top brass, such as the leadership of Force "O"—the lst Division, V Corps (**3-19**).

3-18. Two members of a Navy communications unit scan the horizon out to sea for messages from the ships approaching the shore.

3-19. *(Left to right)* Lieutenant General Bradley, Rear Admiral Hall, Major General Gerow, and Major General Huebner consult while observing the invasion rehearsals off the English coast.

3-20. Destroyer *Thompson* (DD-627) refuels from *Arkansas* during pre-invasion exercises on 21 April 1944. Note the wire, or "hawser," at right securing *Thompson* to the battleship's port beam and refueling line at center.

3-21. *LST-289*, its stern blown away by a torpedo launched in a German E-boat attack on 28 April, lies at Dartmouth, England. An LCM is alongside.

A most important part of the training was refueling at sea (**3-20**). This operation was difficult and dangerous in the stormy waters of the Channel. In addition to such natural hazards and the problems implicit with inexperienced crews, German submarines and E-boats—roughly equivalent to the American motor torpedo boats (MTBs)—posed ever-present dangers.

On 27 April, Assault Force "U" was engaged in Exercise "Tiger" in Lyme Bay. That day all went well, and the only troops left to land at Slapton Sands were those of the follow-up force. That convoy sailed during the evening darkness of 27 April, due to land at 0730 the next day. But at about 0230 on 28 April one—possibly two—of Admiral Krancke's E-boat groups attacked the convoy. The lone escort ship, HMS *Azalea*, was unable to ward off the raid. *LST-507* and *LST-531* were sunk, and *LST-289* was damaged (**3-21**). Casualties were 197 sailors and 441 soldiers—more than the total suffered by the invasion force on D-Day at Utah Beach.

LST-289 was only seven months old when torpedoed. As bad as the damage appears (**3-22**), the LST was repaired, transferred to the British, and eventually sold to the Netherlands, where it was converted to maritime service in 1956.

While all this was going on in southern England, many Americans were stationed in northern Ireland. The battleships *Texas* and *Nevada* were among the ships anchored at Belfast Lough in photo **3-23**, taken on 14 May 1944. Not

3-22. *LST-289*'s badly damaged stern. Note the ship's steel-hulled LCVPs and the cockeyed, single 40mm mount.

3-23. Battleships *Texas* (right) and *Nevada* lie at anchor in Belfast Lough.

3-24. General Eisenhower addresses crew members on the afterdeck of *Texas*.

3-25. Ike and Kirk tour *Quincy* at Belfast Lough.

long thereafter, just prior to the invasion, Eisenhower visited *Texas*. He addressed the crew, who were dressed in blues instead of the standard summer white uniforms. Photo **3-24** shows Rear Admiral Kirk on a platform at the far left. One also sees 40mm AA mounts. On 18 May, Eisenhower and Kirk toured the heavy cruiser *Quincy*, also at Belfast Lough, under the watchful eye of a Marine guard (**3-25**).

Meanwhile, in a Navy hospital in London, medical personnel rehearsed for the inevitable casualties expected to stream back to England in the wake of the invasion (**3-26**).

The paratroopers were equally busy preparing for their anticipated drops behind enemy lines (**3-27**). On 23 March

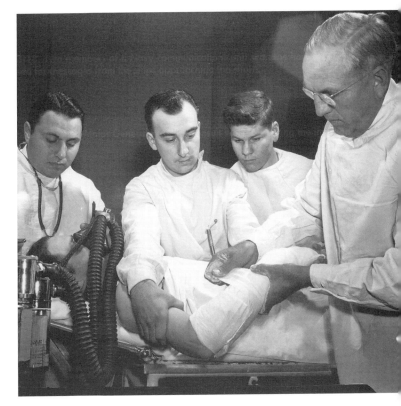

3-26. Anesthetist HA1c Jesse L. Taylor *(left)* concentrates on the "patient," while Capt. A. H. Weiland *(right),* with the assistance of Lt. (jg) Joseph D. Barbella, prepares a plaster bandage for the patient's right forearm. PhM2c Edward G. Schork looks on.

3-27. Members of the Army's 82d Airborne Division display their skills in a demonstration jump.

3-28. Dignitaries including Churchill and Eisenhower watch a practice parachute drop in England on 23 March 1944.

3-29. Members of the 101st Airborne assemble a gun dropped during training exercises in Berkshire, England.

1944, with Churchill and Eisenhower present as interested spectators, the paratroops conducted what was the largest demonstration drop to that date (3-28). Their armament, too, would be air dropped, and those maneuvers also required practice (3-29).

A most important part of the preparations for Overlord was the aerial bombing of the railroads and bridges in northern France. A certain amount of controversy and exhaustive study had preceded the adoption of this policy. Might it not do more harm than good? Of course, it was essential that the Germans be prevented from bringing up troops and matériel faster than the Allies could land their forces; however, previously the plan had been to use the conventional disruptive

pattern of cutting lines, destroying bridges and some important rail points, strafing, and so forth. Nevertheless, Air Chief Marshal Leigh-Mallory proposed an all-out effort to attack not only certain key points, but to saturate the entire rail system. The advantages were obvious, but the disadvantages were unsettling. The bombings would cause massive destruction of French cities and unavoidably heavy losses of French civilians. This aspect particularly troubled the British Parliament. Eventually, the plan was accepted, and the campaign certainly had a tremendous negative effect on the Germans' ability to move up their armor reserves after the initial Normandy landings.

Here we see a medium bomber dropping its bombs during the transportation disruption campaign over France. Some bombs have already exploded near the bridge (3-30). Photo (3-31) shows an actual detonation, and an A-20 is visible at the top of this picture. In photo 3-32 the bombs strike another bridge, but of equal if not more value as a target is the railroad marshaling yard at right. The yards were of critical importance to the Germans, providing space for forming up troop trains and to sort rolling stock. Photo 3-33 shows the result of yet another bridge bombing.

Another of the preparations for Overlord was deception. Patton played a critical role in making the Germans believe that an Allied invasion force would come via the Pas-de-Calais. In the months prior to Overlord, Patton kept a high profile as part of the effort to deceive the Germans. Even after the actual invasion began, Patton's mere presence in the British Isles (and the enemy's healthy respect for that presence) kept the Germans from ruling out a second landing, perhaps at Calais, and further paralyzed the movement of the Wehrmacht's armored reserves.

3-30. Bombs plummet to earth from a Ninth Air Force medium bomber during the railroad- and bridge-busting campaign.

3-31. Bomb detonations temporarily obscure the bridge somewhere in northern France.

3-32. Ninth Air Force bombers attack yet another bridge in northern France.

3-33. Smoldering remains of an additional critical bridge.

Here, in one of the few photos of Patton without a helmet (3-34), the formidable general looks over the engine of a P-51 belonging to the 354th Fighter Group. The 354th was the first fighter group of the Ninth Air Force. Col. George R. Bickell, its commander, was something of a legend in his own right. As a young second lieutenant at Wheeler Field in Hawaii, he had been one of the few USAAF fighter pilots to get airborne on 7 December 1941, albeit after the raid had ended.

Underlying much of the plans and preparations was the need for accurate, current information about defenses. This reconnaissance was an important function of the Ninth Air Force. Its aerial photographs such as 3-35 proved invaluable in determining what to expect in the early hours of the invasion. These reconnaissance flights continued into the early morning hours of 6 June. It was judged significant that

3-34. Lieutenant General Patton inspects the engine of a P-51 at the 354th Fighter Group in the British Isles. At far right is the group commander, Col. George R. Bickell.

3-35. Ninth Air Force reconnaissance photo shows beach obstructions near Cherbourg one month prior to the invasion. Note the Germans standing and, in some cases, running among the obstacles.

3-36. Normandy, 0140, 6 June 1944.

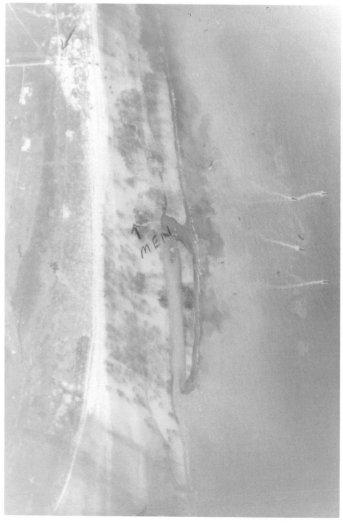

the Germans were effecting no great troop concentrations along the coast. Photographs like **3-36** were made in the dark using an Edgerton flash unit from an altitude of 800 to 2,000 feet. Photo **3-37**, also taken early on 6 June, detected no troop movements near this intersection.

The logistical considerations for supplying entire armies, moving them across the Channel—or just maintaining them in Britain—were staggering. As ton after endless ton of matériel was unloaded, it may well have seemed, as some facetiously remarked, that the British Isles stood in dire danger of sinking beneath the weight. Photo **3-38**, taken in April 1944, pictures a quartermaster yard full of coils of communications cable, while photo **3-39** reveals stocks of oil and other supplies gathered in preparation for the cross-Channel attack.

3-37. Road intersection in northern France, early morning, 6 June 1944.

3-38. Quartermaster Depot G-22 at Moreton-on-Lugg, Hertfordshire, England.

3-39. General Depot G-23 at Histon, England.

CHAPTER 4

Loading Operations and Cross-Channel Voyage

4-1. Lt. Col. D. W. MacArdle admires the handiwork displayed on the back of Sea1c Edwin Parker's jacket during the loading operations just prior to D-Day.

Now the preliminaries were over. Plans, preparations, training, indoctrination, dry runs, exercises, maneuvers—all of these things, however well conceived and earnestly implemented, carried a vague hint of make-believe. Now the real operation was upon them all. The actual invasion was scheduled for 5 June. Loading had begun on 31 May, and since 3 June vessels had been moving toward their assembly points, ready to join their respective convoys. There would be no celebratory send-off; the forces would have to move as secretly as possible considering their massive nature. For the officers and men, quiet good-byes would be exchanged between newfound friends.

The inevitable touches of bravado surfaced. Here (4-1) Lt. Col. D. W. MacArdle examines a sailor's decorated jacket. Was the "LuLu" thus honored the sailor's girl back home, or did he wistfully wish she were? Or was she a fantasy?

D-Day would be well authenticated, for artists, photographers, and correspondents for various media were landing with the assault troops. These men were as brave as any combatant; they knew German mines and bullets were indifferent to the status of their victims. In photo 4-2 a Navy combat artist is hard at work. A reporter for the Blue Radio Network, George Hicks, his identifying correspondent patch on his left arm, kept busy interviewing Navy men (4-3).

By 1 June, Force "B," or the Backup Force, under Commodore Edgar was ready to begin loading from Falmouth and Fowey. Photo 4-4 gives an idea of the activity with LCVPs circling in the background. At right is the heavy cruiser USS *Augusta* (CA-31), flagship of the Western Naval Task Force. The Canadian destroyer HMCS *Huron* (not a part of the Normandy-bound fleet) is moored at left with three other

4-2. Lt. Comdr. Dwight Shepler sketches an LST in the background.

4-3. Correspondent George Hicks records interviews with men on board an LST before the Normandy invasion. Note the electronics gear in the foreground.

4-4. Men of Force "B" (Backup Force) line up on the docks in Plymouth, England, to commence loading operations on 1 or 2 June.

Tribal-class sisters. In photo **4-5** we see two Force "B" LCVPs prepare to transfer men aboard a larger ship. *LCI-403*, *LCI-538*, and *LCI-537* are in the background.

Rear Admiral Hall's Assault Force "O" assembled at Poole, Weymouth, and Portland Harbor before organizing in nine convoys (**4-6**). The latter point was particularly busy, with a steady stream of men and vehicles pouring in. By a near-miracle of organization, the traffic kept moving toward the assigned craft. Portland Harbor was scheduled to be cleared by 0315 on 4 June. The British and Canadians, too, were assembling their Assault Forces "G," "J," and "S" into 16, 10, and 12, respectively, convoys from Portsmouth, the Solent, and Spithead.

Among the troops embarking were those of the 116th Infantry Regiment, 1st Battalion, headed for Beaches Dog and Easy Green on Omaha Beach as part of Assault Force "O-2" (**4-7**). Normally the 116th was assigned to the 29th Division, but it was temporarily assigned to the 1st Infantry Division from 17 May to 7 June. Unhappily, many of these men would not live to see the sunrise of 7 June.

Some of the cameramen photographing the action froze in time little, personal vignettes—an Army captain clinging to the port side of an LCVP during unloading, a sailor with the name "Blasen" stenciled on his jacket (**4-8**).

4-5. Two Force "B" LCVPs in Plymouth come alongside a larger ship to transfer their men on board.

4-7. Members of the 116th Infantry Regiment, 1st Battalion, depart from the beach in a fully laden LCVP, bound for the USS *Thomas Jefferson* (APA-30). Note inflatable life belt on soldier at right.

4-6. Assault Force "O," lying at Portland Harbor, England, readies itself on 2 June for the voyage to Omaha Beach.

4-8. Troops transfer from an LCVP to *LCI(L)-539*. Rations are piled on the LCI's deck.

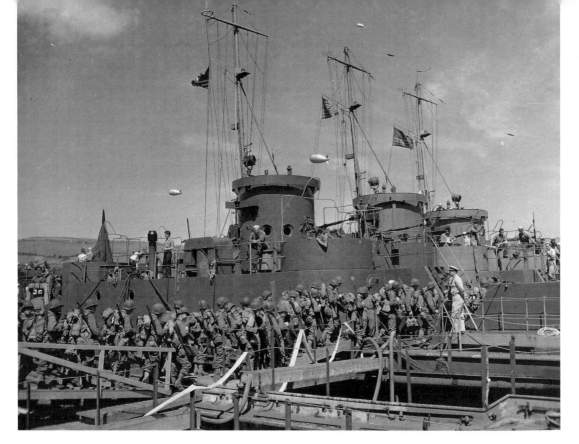

In some cases, troops could board from a dock rather than transferring from a smaller craft (**4-9**). Matériel as well as men poured aboard (**4-10** and **4-11**).

Rear Admiral Moon's Assault Force "U" loaded at five ports and would embark from eight, including Dartmouth, Salcombe, and Torquay, while formed in twelve convoys. Photo **4-12** gives a glimpse of some of the men and craft belonging to Force "O" Task Unit 125.5.3. Under the command of Lt. Comdr. R. G. Newbegin, this unit would assault Red Beach. "Lead, direct, or get out of the way!" seemed to be the watchword as one vehicle after another rolled aboard the waiting vessels (**4-13**).

4-10. Trucks destined for Omaha Beach back into *LST-51* at Portland Harbor, England, on 2 June 1944. The truck backing in is a British Bedford with American wheels.

4-11. View from *LST-51* as it backs away from its mooring at Portland Harbor on 2 June. *LST-75* is in the background at left, with a barrage balloon flying above it.

4-12. Laden with troops bound for Utah Beach, an LCVP approaches a nest of LCIs belonging to Task Unit 125.5.3.

4-13. An Army captain guides vehicles assigned to Force "U" on board *LCT-821* at Dartmouth, England, on 1 June 1944. Note M-7 Priest self-propelled howitzers among the cargo.

4-14. An Army Field Kitchen Unit rolls on board *LST-506*. Note cartoon painted on the side of the kitchen unit. Just to the left rear of the kitchen, a sailor named "Dick" looks on.

4-15. Utah Beach–bound M-16 gun motor carriage boards *LST-47* at Dartmouth on 1 June. Note famed "quad-.50s" mount in half-track at left and the nickname "Der Fuehrer's Express."

The field kitchen shown in photo **4-14** serves as a reminder that, unlike most invaders in history, the U.S. Army would not live off the land, not even of its enemies. It fed its own, and while griping about the food was a standing operating procedure, those field kitchens would be exceedingly reassuring.

In photos **4-15** and **4-16** we see the loading aboard *LST-47* of a vehicle nicknamed "Der Fuehrer's Express." Photo **4-17** shows the next step in the adventures of "Der Fuehrer's Express" as *LST-47* on 2 June awaits the signal to set sail for Normandy.

4-16. View of loading from hold of *LST-47*. "Der Fuehrer's Express" backs in.

4-17. Lying in the River Dart, *LST-47* (no doubt with "Der Fuehrer's Express" safely tucked away on board).

4-18. Chaplain Meyer holds Jewish services on board *Ancon*, flagship of Force "O," in early June.

During World War I, it was frequently said, "There are no atheists in foxholes." Evidently there were few aboard the ships awaiting the signal to get under way, either. Many men wondered what, if anything, would come next if this would in fact be their last voyage. No doubt many attended the services of three faiths held aboard the Force "O" flagship *Ancon* (**4-18, 4-19,** and **4-20**). All three of these pictures were taken in the same location, with the same rug and same altar in use—an example of practical ecumenism that might be rare in civilian life but was quite common in camp and aboard ship. Services were held aboard small as well as large vessels (**4-21**).

While the men went through their private rituals, top brass met twice a day at Admiral Ramsay's headquarters to evaluate the one factor they could not control—the weather. At these meetings, the center of attention was neither Ramsay nor Eisenhower, but an RAF weather officer, Group Capt. J. M. Stagg. British weather forecasting was more reliable than that of the Germans, who received no firm information from farther east than Norway. And what

4-19. Catholic Chaplain Deery conducts Mass on *Ancon.*

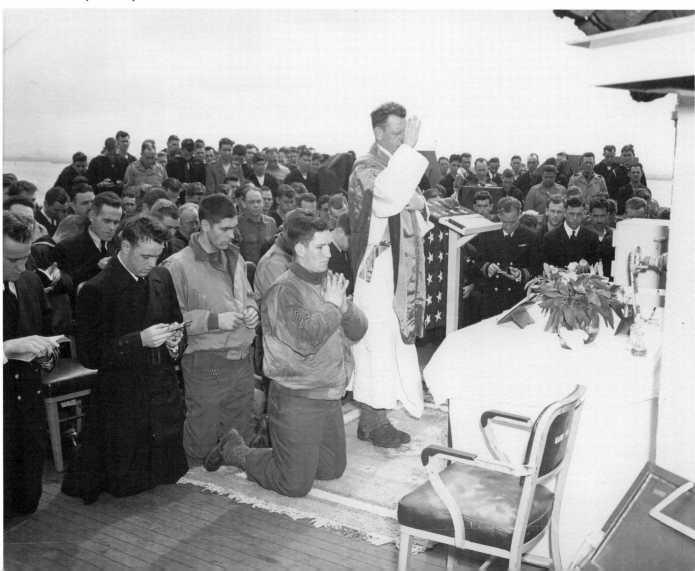

4-20. Protestant services in progress on *Ancon* on 3 June. Seated in the front row, Generals Gerow and Huebner seek reassurance from Navy Chaplain R. H. McConnell. Note V Corps patch on shoulder of man at right.

the British knew was not reassuring. Even in the pleasant month of June they would have only two three-day periods that would be satisfactory for the invasion when considering tidal conditions, daylight, and the moon. One of these windows was 5–7 June; the other, 18–20 June.

The selected invasion date was the fifth. By the early hours of 3 June the prospects looked dangerous, but Eisenhower, knowing the disadvantages of postponement, allowed plans to go forward. The weather picture grew steadily worse, however, and at the meeting of 0400 on Sunday, 4 June, it became obvious that the overcast sky would ground the supporting air attack and heavy seas would overpower landing craft. Predictably, Montgomery wanted to go ahead, regardless of the weather, but everyone else favored bowing to the elements. Ike agreed. He postponed the operation for one day.

The general signal for postponement was given at 0515 on 4 June, though the ships were recalled to their emergency postponement ports at 0500. The Force "U" convoys, having the farthest to go, had already set sail during the afternoon of 3 June and had to be recalled, along with Force "O," which had sortied later. All of the convoys save one were back in port by 2240 on 4 June.

Crowded into small beaching craft in a driving downpour and no doubt feeling let down at this latest manifestation of "hurry up and wait," the soldiers sat out the day. No less uncomfortable were the top brass, but theirs was the discomfort of almost unbearable tension. Would the weather break?

4-21. Catholic services on a Coast Guard–manned LCI.

4-22. *Dorothea L. Dix* (APA-67) of Assault Force "O-3," Comdr. William I. Leahy commanding, lies at anchor on 5 June, following the postponement of 4 June. Embarking a portion of the 16th Infantry Regiment of the 1st Division, this unit would be first in at Omaha, on Beaches Fox Green and Easy Red.

By 2115 on 4 June Stagg had relatively good news. Although the overall weather picture was still bad, he foresaw a break in the storm on 6 June. A decision was postponed in deference to Leigh-Mallory, who was pessimistic about the air operations. After a final weather conference in the wee hours of 5 June, Ike made his historic decision at 0415: "OK, we'll go."

Once more the ships became arenas of action, and the men were itching to go. Photos **4-22** and **4-23** show typical scenes of this period. Once more religious services were held, utilizing any available space as the men prepared themselves for battle. Classical music buffs might have been reminded of "Put on the armor of light" from Mendelssohn's cantata, "St. Paul" (**4-24** and **4-25**).

4-23. An LCVP plies its way toward a transport on 5 June off the coast of England.

4-24. Army Chaplain Edward R. Waters holds services on a pier. Note profusion of inflatable life belts and the soldier "Jersey" with a drawing of a jeep on the back of his jacket in foreground.

4-25. An Anglican priest pronounces a benediction upon the crew of HMCS *Algonquin* on 5 June. A destroyer in Force "J" of the Eastern Task Force, *Algonquin* was destined for the Canadian Juno Beach landings in Normandy.

4-26. On 5 June Coast Guard Coxswain Don D. Brewer finds time to send home one last letter before the invasion. Note pictures of wife or sweetheart and the pipe tobacco on the shelf behind him and the pinup on the wall.

Amid such chores as last-minute checks of equipment, many took the occasion to send what might be a last letter to loved ones at home, some taking advantage of the convenient and popular V-Mail (4-26, 4-27, and 4-28).

Ike left his headquarters late on 5 June to send off the troops. In one of the classic war photographs of all time (4-29), Ike meets and talks with men of the 101st Airborne Division. Other members of the 101st read mail from home—their last letters before the invasion and the last occasion for a smile many would have (4-30). Lieutenant General Brereton, in command of the Ninth Air Force, also visited the 101st Airborne (4-31 and 4-32). The C-47s of his IX Transport Command would be dropping these men over France.

4-27. Shortly before embarking on C-47 transports, members of Col. Leroy Lindquist's 508th Parachute Infantry, 82d Airborne Division, receive V-Mail blanks in order to send one last letter to wives, sweethearts, or the folks at home.

4-28. Other members of the 508th check equipment at their temporary airfield at Saltby, England.

4-29. Eisenhower talks to troops of the 101st Airborne Division shortly before their departure. Purpose of the "23" sign on the man at right is a mystery.

4-30. Members of the 101st Airborne Division, with camouflage on their helmets and face darkened, read one last letter from home.

4-32. Soldier at left in the previous picture manages a smile for the camera.

4-31. Lieutenant General Brereton, commanding general, Ninth Air Force, bids farewell to members of the 101st Airborne. Note the very roughly and, likely, hurriedly painted invasion stripes on the fuselage of the C-47 in the background.

4-33. Medical evacuation teams prepare to load up for Normandy on the evening of 5 June. Note their Red Cross armbands and aircraft invasion stripes.

4-34. Army troops on board a Force "U" LCT stand ready for the ride across the English Channel to Utah Beach.

4-35. A Coast Guard–manned LST departs from England on the voyage to Normandy.

Now movement began in earnest (**4-33** and **4-34**). In the latter photo some wear 4th Infantry Division "Ivy" shoulder patches. At least one man is in the 101st Airborne. Note the carton of Lucky Strike cigarettes in the backpack of the soldier in the bottom of the photo.

Several items of interest and typical of the operation appear in photo **4-35**. A signaler is at work, with a radar dish behind him. A British Army sergeant stands in back of the truck at right. The bundle of sticks atop one of the trucks halfway down on the right will be used to fashion a roadway through the Norman sand dunes (see **6-35**). In photos **4-36, 4-37,** and **4-38** we see LCIs and a Rhino ferry in the course of the journey.

At the time, any literate English-speaking individual could scarcely fail to be reminded of Henry V's invasion fleet, "A city on th'inconstant billows dancing." But, as Morison pointed out, the Overlord ships held more men than did any city in Shakespeare's day, and more vessels were headed for Normandy than existed in the whole world when the Bard wrote of Henry's invasion.

Despite the size and complexity of the operation, it went off amazingly well. The billows were "inconstant" enough, but no vessel, however small, was lost, and they were very close to schedule timewise. Most surprising of all, the Germans did not detect the invaders. The E-boats had not been sent out on patrol, because the weather was considered too foul and the tides "not right."

4-36. A convoy of LCIs sails across the English Channel toward Normandy on D-Day. A barrage balloon protects each LCI from low-flying aircraft.

4-37. Heavily laden Rhino ferry *RHF-3* makes the final leg of the journey toward the invasion beaches, while a Coast Guard rescue boat is in the distance. The name "Hell's Angels" appears on the barge at right.

4-38. A convoy of LCIs as seen from the Force "O" flagship *Ancon*. Note the 20mm mounts on *Ancon* and the variety of headgear the men are wearing.

CHAPTER 5 | D-Day: 6 June 1944

Omaha Beach comprised an area between Utah Beach and the British Gold sector. Geographically it began at the base of the Cotentin peninsula from the border between Manche and Calvados to the shore about three miles from Port-en-Bessin-Huppain, where Gold began. The topography was unpromising at best. While Omaha's bluffs and wide, sandy beaches were an improvement over the cliffs and narrow, pebble beaches on either side, the territory was still more favorable to the defenders than to the invaders. The latter had to cross about 300 yards of wet beach, a narrow expense of dry sand, and then a single seawall. Then came an artificial seawall protected by barbed wire. Beyond that came a grassy area, then a line of bluffs that, except for a few ravines, defied vehicles.

The whole area offered no cover and, contrary to Allied intelligence, was well defended. Although the Germans might be fixated—understandably enough—on Pas-de-Calais as an invasion site and they might be keeping a wary eye on Patton, they knew that the Normandy coast was another possible area of invasion, even if only a secondary one. So, in addition to facing natural handicaps, the U.S. landing parties would have to contend with several layers of artificial obstacles. And after they ran that gauntlet, these invaders would come up against over two regiments of excellent German troops. In fact, to quote Morison, "the Germans had provided the best imitation of hell for an invading force that American troops had encountered anywhere."

British and Canadian minesweepers had been at work clearing the approaches from a few minutes after midnight 5 June until shortly after sunrise and, surprisingly, encountered no enemy fire. Next came the fire support, divided into two groups. *Arkansas* headed the eastern group (5-1). The British heavy cruiser HMS *Glasgow* led the western group, followed by *Texas* (5-2). These two fire support groups also included eight American destroyers, three British destroyers, and two French light cruisers, *Montcalm* and *Georges Leygues*, which followed *Arkansas* (5-3 to 5-5).

5-1. *Arkansas* bombards the French coastline in support of the landings at Omaha Beach. Note the immense cloud of black smoke from the battleship's main battery of twelve 12-inch guns.

5-2. Bombardment in the vicinity of Pointe du Hoc, as seen from the battleship *Texas*. Note the church steeple and the buildings high atop the bluffs. This village is likely St. Pierre-du-Mont.

5-3. Farther down the coast, an American destroyer passes between *Texas* and the coastline.

5-4. Destroyer USS *Harding* (DD-625) stands guard over landing craft making their runs onto Omaha Beach. Note the destroyer's main battery turned to port and the explosion in the center of the picture. Smoke rising behind the coastline lends further evidence of the bombardment.

5-5. *Georges Leygues* or *Montcalm* provides gunfire support for the invading troops. A *Gleaves*-class destroyer in the background at left.

5-6. The troops go in. Landing craft lumber past *Augusta*, flagship of the Western Naval Task Force. That *Augusta*'s main battery is not turned shoreward was likely *not* a consolation to the men in the landing craft.

5-7. With heavy smoke on shore drifting to the east, *LCC-449* and *LCG-424*, British vessels under the U.S. flag, lend support to the landing operations on Omaha Beach.

The transports began anchoring at 0251, eleven miles out. This spot had been chosen to keep the ships beyond the range of the guns at Pointe du Hoc, but it turned out to be a sad miscalculation. In the first place, Pointe du Hoc did not have heavy guns. Second, this long distance from shore left the smaller landing craft at the mercy of the wind and waves as indicated by the choppy water and splashes thrown up by the leading craft in the foreground of photo **5-6**.

Meanwhile, the bombardment continued, not only from battleships, carriers, or destroyers. British LCGs (landing craft, gun) under the American flag provided the first support closer to the beaches than the deeper-draft ships could approach (**5-7**).

During the morning hours of the Omaha Beach operation, it seemed that everything that could go wrong did and that disaster waited to pounce. Scheduled to land from LSTs a few minutes in advance of the troops, to provide fire cover,

were the DD (dual-drive amphibious) tanks. In most cases, however, they proved somewhat less than amphibious when their flotation equipment failed. The officer in charge of their western group was wisely reluctant to trust the DD tanks to the rough seas three miles off the beach and sought permission to land them instead. But in the eastern sector, they went overboard as planned, and only five out of thirty-two reached land. Following their eleven-mile voyage through heavy seas in small craft, the troops landed exhausted, soaking, and seasick. Nevertheless, the first waves reached the beaches almost on time (**5-8** and **5-9**).

Confusion dogged the operation. The wind and tide pulled a number of craft off course, and at roughly 500 yards offshore, German fire ranging from small arms to artillery made progress very difficult indeed. In photo **5-10** an LVCP from *Samuel Chase* smokes after a German machine-gun bullet strikes a hand grenade. The boat's coxswain, Coast

5-8. Two landing craft, *LCI-490* and *LCI-496*, prepare to make the last dash to the beach. Note heavy smoke on shore.

5-9. LCVPs crowded with infantry from Assault Force "O-1" press toward Beaches Fox Red and Easy Green. The LCVP at far left is from the transport *Samuel Chase* (APA-26). Note the large waves the landing craft churned up and the ubiquitous smoke on the beach.

5-10. An LCVP from *Samuel Chase* charges ahead despite the explosion of a hand grenade on board after a German machine-gun bullet finds its mark.

5-11. The view from inside an LCVP heading toward Omaha Beach. The men's attention seems to be directed at something happening off the craft's port side.

5-12. American soldiers of the 1st Infantry Division reopen the Western Front against Hitler's Wehrmacht.

5-13. Somewhat later in the morning, troops disembark from *LCI-553* onto Omaha Beach.

Guardsman Delba L. Nivens, put out the fire with the aid of his engineman and was able to nurse the craft back to its mother ship. The men aboard another LCVP (**5-11**) must have found its NO SMOKING sign ludicrous. Most are armed with M-1 carbines, although the soldier at the far left has the heavier M-1 rifle.

These weapons soon proved to be at best a mixed blessing. The landing craft began disembarking the men at 0630 about 50 to 100 yards offshore, where the water was three to four feet deep. The men's weapons and heavy packs weighed them down as effectively as an anchor. Many drowned after receiving what on shore would have been a slight wound or even a fall. For those who slogged grimly on, the beach must have looked immeasurably far off, and even when they arrived, it offered little or no shelter (**5-12**). To make matters worse, many company grade officers were killed, leaving the men of this first wave without adequate leadership. However, the men of the 1st Infantry Division had achieved their mission: they reopened the Western Front.

Optimists hoped for a smooth, efficient operation, moving in accordance with plans and training, but bad luck pursued the men's every step. Of eight companies, only two landed on their assigned beaches. Casualties among company grade officers continued to be horrendous, and German fire was both heavy and effective. Morison described the scene: "All along Omaha there was a disunited, confused and partly leaderless body of infantry, without cohesion, with no artillery support, huddled under the seawall to get shelter from the withering fire."

Two shells hit *LCI-553*, pictured in **5-13**, and the next day she was left on the beach as a wreck. This unfortunate craft can be seen at the upper left of photo **5-14**, which shows troops of Assault Force "O-1" landing some one hundred yards down the beach in the eastern sector. Trucks and DUKWs were beginning to collect on the beach. Such was the congestion that at 0830 the Omaha beach master called

a halt to vehicle landings, but troops continued to pour in.

By 1000 Omaha was in deep trouble. Bradley, aboard *Augusta*, sent Maj. Chester Hansen ashore for a firsthand report. Around 1130 he returned with a grim picture. Three assault waves were bottlenecked behind the first. Most of the men were pinned down by the defenders' fire; dead and wounded men and ruined vehicles littered the beach. So far as he could tell, no progress had been made in scaling the bluffs. Actually, a few groups of not more than ten men had begun to move in that direction—the first sign that the tide had turned.

But at noon the situation was still so questionable that Bradley seriously considered writing off Omaha and diverting the remaining troops and matériel to Gold Beach. Twenty-five thousand men and forty-four hundred vehicles awaited the second tide of 6 June to reach Omaha's transport area. Should he permit them to land? It was one of those questions that answers itself, however agonizingly. To give up on Omaha would mean isolating Utah Beach and the British sector, wasting the lives already spent, and abandoning thousands more. The three sectors were parts of an indissoluble whole. This battle had no thinkable alternative; the invasion, once begun, had to continue with all parts in place.

Gradually the sheer force of numbers began to tell as the later troops started to come in. Men landing in the afternoon could see broached tracks and troops pinned down on the shore. The gunner in the 20mm tub on the bow of *LCI-412* engaged the enemy as the craft moved toward the beach that afternoon (**5-15**).

By midday troops ashore were beginning to make a little headway, starting with their advance inward. The White M-3 half-tracks with artillery pieces and DUKWs shown in photo **5-16** seem to be having a better time of it than those in the previous picture. Still, Army artillery played almost no part in the D-Day activities, and the soldiers had good

5-14. A portion of Assault Force "O-1" splashes ashore from landing craft onto Easy Red or Fox Green. LCVP at left is from *Samuel Chase*.

5-15. Troops disembark from *LCI-412* via ladders on either side of bow during the afternoon of 6 June.

5-16. Soldiers wade ashore from another LCVP.

5-17. *LCI-538* (also seen in photo 4-5) unloads the Force "B" reinforcements, who started landing at about 1630 onto Omaha Beach. Obstructions in the surf can be seen behind the troops.

cause to be thankful for the U.S. Navy's firepower. As the day brightened, first destroyers and later the battleships shelled German gun positions. Thanks in no small part to Navy firepower, that afternoon Army losses in men and matériel—though still high—were considerably lower than in the morning.

The next three photos provide a glimpse of the action from *LCI-538*. An Army photographer captured the view from Omaha Beach as the landing craft began to unload Force "B" reinforcements around 1630 (**5-17**). Burdened with rifles, bazookas, ammunition boxes, and wet uniforms, these men slog ashore (**5-18**). The soldier carrying the rocket launcher has just passed to the left as another man, wearing a life belt, moves into the camera's view (**5-19**). Wherever one looked, the scene was grim and dreary, illuminated only by the quiet splendor of men doing their unpleasant duty as best they could. And what no photograph can show, the noise was deafening.

Landings continued. Another platoon, armed with a mixture of M-1 carbines and rifles, plodded toward shore (**5-20**).

5-18. Force "B" troops in their wet uniforms plod ashore burdened with weapons and equipment. One of the soldiers directly in front of *LCI-538* carried an M-1A1 rocket launcher with flash deflector attached.

5-19. The soldier carrying the rocket launcher has just passed to the left, as another man wearing an inflatable life belt trudges toward the camera.

5-20. Another platoon splashes through the surf during late afternoon of D-Day. The soldier at left has another M-1A1 rocket launcher.

5-21. *LST-21* unloads British trucks and tanks including a Sherman nicknamed "Virgin" at left. Note that the Royal Navy sailor on the barge at left wears the same type of horizontal band on his helmet as do U.S. Navy personnel.

Simultaneous with the landings at Omaha, U.S. Coast Guard–manned LSTs off-loaded in areas farther to the west. In **5-21**, *LST-21* goes about that business.

And still they came—here men of Assault Group "O-3," 16th Infantry Regiment, 3d Battalion, assemble at Fox Green, Omaha, while *LCI-83* unloads more men. This regiment led the assault on Omaha. There was no seawall for protection at Fox Green, as attested by the casualties and debris (**5-22**). Here a man of the 3d Battalion crouches miserably under a blanket, near a life belt and what appears to be a battle casualty (**5-23**).

5-22. Part of Assault Group "O-3," 16th Infantry Regiment, 3d Battalion, assembles on a narrow strip on the gravelly beach at Fox Green, Omaha. This photo was taken near Colleville-sur-Mer.

5-23. A 3d Battalion man, cold, wet, and exhausted, huddles under a blanket on Fox Green. (An Army photographer named Hall took this and the next four poignant photos.)

Some 3d Battalion casualties were given food and cigarettes and prepared for evacuation to England (**5-24**). But others would have to remain in Normandy, except in the memory of those who loved them (**5-25**). Some, not seriously wounded, received first aid promptly (**5-26**). All wounded, American or German, were given first aid. In photo **5-27** an American captain bandages the hand of an infantry *obergefreiter*, or corporal.

Photo **5-28** records a dismal scene of beach obstructions, wrecked trucks, and a bogged-down tank. By 0800, not a single man or vehicle had moved off the beaches in the western area. As mentioned, at 0830 the congestion was such that the beach master suspended further unloading. At last, however, the situation began to settle down as the men started to move inland (**5-29**).

5-24. Third Battalion casualties await evacuation to England.

5-25. Five soldiers from the 1st Division, 16th Infantry Regiment, 3d Battalion, who would not go home.

5-26. An American medical officer bandages the hand of a soldier near Colleville-sur-Mer, Omaha Beach.

5-27. An *obergefreiter* (corporal) from General Kraiss's 352d Division has his hand bandaged by an American captain. The white piping on the German's shoulder straps denotes infantry.

5-28. American equipment litters Omaha Beach on the afternoon of 6 June.

5-29. American assault troops set up a command and information post beside a silent enemy pillbox. Note the fragmentation damage to the exterior of the pillbox.

5-30. Just out of the surf, a wounded soldier from Force "B" receives a plasma transfusion.

All progress was at a heavy cost although, as noted before, the worst casualties occurred in the morning. The long shadows in photo **5-30** indicate that it was late afternoon when this soldier from the 5th Engineer Special Brigade of Force "B" received a plasma transfusion. All too many were beyond help. The crossed rifles in photo **5-31** signify the presence of a dead infantryman. As daylight waned, bodies awaiting burial or evacuation were an all-too-common sight (**5-32**).

The action at Pointe du Hoc deserves special attention. "Hoc" is Old French for "jib" and has been consistently misspelled in books and reports. This point is a triangular cape that rises in a sheer cliff some 117 feet from a shore consisting of large rocks (**5-33**). Also visible are craters from shelling—probably from *Texas*'s 14-inch salvos—and the rope ladders fired by LCA (landing craft, assault) rocket launchers.

5-31. Crossed rifles lie beside an American who perished on Omaha Beach in 6 June assault. Note the obstruction on the beach and the life belt around the soldier, who had taken shrapnel in his right leg.

5-32. The scene on either Fox Green or Easy Red, Omaha Beach, in the aftermath of the 6 June assault. Bodies and a large pile of inflatable life belts are at upper right.

The Germans had placed a battery of six 155mm guns, two of them in casemates, on this western edge of Omaha Beach. With the enemy so totally commanding the invasion beaches, it was considered impossible for the landings to succeed without the guns being first taken out of action—hence the mission given to two hundred men of the 2d Ranger Battalion, led by Lt. Col. James A. Rudder. To be sure, there were those who doubted that the Rangers could carry it off. Admiral Hall's intelligence officer stated that "three old women with brooms could keep the Rangers from climbing that cliff."

The Rangers were to land in twelve British LCAs (its speed, six knots). Half of the LCAs were fitted with rocket launchers, out of which were fired lines, grappling hooks,

5-33. A landing craft unloads supplies (possibly from the BB *Texas*) for the Ranger battalions on Pointe du Hoc.

5-34. U.S. Army Rangers scale the rough terrain of Pointe du Hoc. An extension ladder is visible on the face of the cliff.

and rope ladders. LCAs also carried light section ladders and other ladders borrowed from, of all places, the London Fire Department. After a 35-minute delay caused by mistaking Pointe de la Perce for the objective, the Rangers landed in broad daylight (**5-34**) faced by angry German soldiers who had been awakened by the early morning bombardment from the destroyer *Satterlee* (DD-626). The destroyer gamely kept most of the Germans at bay while the Rangers scaled the cliffs (**5-35** and **5-36**). The DUKWs carrying the fire ladders could not ascend the steep, rocky beach, but the extension ladders and rocket-propelled lines did work. Within 30 minutes, the Rangers had scaled the cliffs, only to discover the "guns" were merely telephone poles, temporarily in place during casemate construction.

5-35. Rangers show off the line and ladders used to scale the heights on Pointe du Hoc.

5-36. With his shoulder patch proudly proclaiming his status as a Ranger, the soldier at right reloads a clip for his M-1 carbine.

Though the Rangers were quite isolated, they soon received sorely needed reinforcements to cope with the opposition, largely those German gunners who were quartered in underground galleries.

While one contingent of Rangers held the Pointe, another group pushed out to the Grandcamp-Vierville Road. One patrol actually discovered four of the six guns supposed to be at the Pointe, concealed in a field commanding Utah Beach. With the spiking and disabling of these guns, the Rangers' primary mission was completed.

All during the day, destroyers *Satterlee*, *Barton* (DD-722), and *Thompson* (see **3-20**) lent fire support. Rudder's situation grew critical as the day wore on. Only half of his men were fit to fight by the morning of 7 June. Admiral Bryant sent in food and ammunition to the beach from *Texas* to keep the Rangers fighting (**5-37**). Finally, on 8 June, the Rangers were relieved by the 116th Infantry Regiment of the 29th Division, after control of that unit was passed back from the 1st Division on 7 June.

5-37. Lt. Comdr. John K. Knapper of the battleship *Texas* and a companion examine a German pillbox on Pointe du Hoc on 6 June, possibly during efforts of that ship to resupply the Rangers. Knapper had served aboard *Texas* since joining it as an ensign in 1939. Note the belted German ammunition at left and a dead Ranger covered up at right.

5-38. *Nevada* (BB-36) bombards Utah Beach with its 14-inch guns in support of the VII Corps landings.

5-39. *Nevada's* forward guns belch smoke and flame during the bombardment. Note the camouflage paint on the gun barrels.

5-40. During the morning of 6 June, a shell from the German counterbattery fire on Utah Beach explodes on St.-Marcouf Island. This and the next view were photographed from the heavy cruiser *Quincy* (CA-71).

UTAH BEACH

This sector ran roughly from the Omaha area up to the Cotentin peninsula to the town of Quineville. In contrast to Omaha, Utah had no bluffs or cliffs to impede progress; it was simply a beach and must have looked familiar to any soldier or sailor who had seen the mid-Atlantic coast of the United States. First came a long expanse of sand some 400 yards wide at low tide. This tidal beach blended into a shallow expanse of dry sand with the usual accumulation of driftwood and seaweed. Then came about 150 yards of sand dunes and beach grass. Here, facing the sea, the Germans had built a low wall of concrete. They had also strewn antiboat obstacles across the tidal sand. Two natural offshore obstacles were the banks of Cardonnet and St.-Marcouf and

two islets also named St.-Marcouf.

Thanks in part to this topography, the action at Utah went off much more smoothly and at considerably less cost than at Omaha. Timing was particularly smooth. Admiral Moon's flagship *Bayfield* and the other transports reached their destinations at the planned time. Admirals Deyo and Moon and General Collins had quite an accurate idea of the extent and location of the German defenses.

Off-loading the transports began at 0405, some 11.5 miles from Utah's high-water mark. An hour later, German guns opened up, and at about 0530, Deyo gave the order for the pre-landing bombardment (5-38 and 5-39). The Americans expected the St.-Marcouf Islands to be fortified, but the Germans had neglected that precaution; in fact, on at least one occasion the German batteries shelled them (5-40). Meanwhile, as they had before the disembarking,

minesweepers would have to clear the way (**5-41**). Farther in toward shore, destroyers attacked the German beach fortifications (**5-42** and **5-43**).

The long run in choppy waters from the transports (**5-44**) to shore was difficult for the men, but twenty landing craft reached the shore at H-hour, 0630, on the dot (**5-45**). But if the time was right, the place obviously was not (**5-46** and **5-47**). The terrain did not agree with the charts. Brig. Gen. Theodore Roosevelt, with his detailed knowledge of the terrain gleaned from painstaking study of maps, soon determined what had happened. Somehow the force had landed around 2,000 yards south of the planned locale. He persuaded the naval officer in charge to divert other landing

5-41. Minesweepers working to clear shipping channels explode mines in the waters across Cardonnet Bank.

5-42. *Gleaves*-class destroyer throws 5-inch shells into the beach fortifications at Normandy.

5-43. Expended 5-inch/.38-caliber cartridge cases litter the deck of USS *Hobson* (DD-464).

5-44. Force "U" is under way. *Bayfield* lowers its LCVPs into the water. *Nevada* just to the left of *Bayfield*.

5-45. Lt. Abe Condiotti, U.S. Naval Reserve (USNR), credited with commanding the first boat to hit Utah Beach about 0630 on 6 June.

5-46. American soldiers with full equipment leap into the surf and wade toward Utah Beach near Les Dunes de Madeleine. This particular load includes a number of medics. The horizontal lozenge on the back of the helmet denotes an NCO so that the men could recognize their leaders from the rear. Handles of a stretcher protrude into photo at left. (This and the next photo were taken by Army photographer Shelton.)

5-47. The camera looks up just as the NCOs in the previous picture exit the landing craft. A number of vehicles have already landed.

craft to this new location. The mistake could not have been more fortunate. Providence—or luck—had moved the landing site from a heavily defended sector to one that was almost unprotected (**5-48**).

Of course, Utah was not casualty-free (**5-49** and **5-50**), but by comparison with Omaha, the cost was light. By 0945, fifteen waves had landed and were beginning to move inland (**5-51** and **5-52**). By 1800, according to Mori-

5-48. Viewed from a landing craft, a weapons carrier charges ashore at Utah Beach. Note the machine gun on the weapons carrier and the other vehicles on the beach.

5-49. Members of the American landing party assist survivors of a sunken landing craft. One of the survivors at center with an inflated life belt helps pull to shore a comrade, who looks somewhat the worse for wear and may be wounded. An NCO and a beach landing-party member assist another survivor *(left)*; one soldier *(left center)* refuses to put down his M-1 rifle; and a third survivor *(right)* trudges ashore wearily on his own power.

5-50. First aid being administered to soldiers on Utah Beach. The survivors have collapsed on the beach and are covered with blankets. The soldier still clutching his M-1 now stands off at left. Note *LCM-29* unloading in the background. (This and the previous photo in this rescue sequence were recorded by Army photographer Weintraub, whose name shows up on many Signal Corps photos.)

5-51. Men of the 8th Infantry Regiment, 4th Division, moved out over the seawall at Utah Beach. Men rest or take cover behind the wall, where most have stowed their equipment.

5-52. A German soldier with hobnailed boots and a coverall over his uniform lies dead beside a pillbox near Les Dunes de Madeleine.

son, 21,328 troops, 1,742 vehicles, and 1,695 tons of supplies had been landed on Utah. Organization was effective, with almost no congestion. Many units had left the beach area behind and had entered the Normandy countryside. The following series of photographs (**5-53, 5-54, 5-55,** and **5-56**) give some idea of their progress. A pathetic feature is the dead animals—innocent victims of war.

5-53. Men of the 8th Infantry Regiment, 4th Division, occupy a French village just off Utah Beach. The lead man is still wearing his inflatable life belt.

5-54. Other men of the 4th Division (probably 3d Battalion, 22d Infantry Regiment) occupy a farmyard near Les Dunes de Varreville, two miles northwest of Utah Beach, after clearing German snipers from the buildings.

5-55. The troops shown above take a breather in the milk house of the same farm after clearing out snipers.

5-56. A heavy weapons unit of the 358th Infantry Regiment, 90th Division, pause during its advance inland from Red Beach. The 90th Division patch on the sergeant in the foreground has been censored out. Note the German minefield sign at right. A mortar man heads the column on the left-hand side of the road. The man standing in the road behind the sergeant is part of the beach landing party, as designated by the semicircle painted on his helmet. This is a rare photo of this division on D-Day. This regiment and the 343d Field Artillery Battalion were the only contingents of the 90th Division to land on 6 June. The rest followed on 7–8 June.

5-57. A Coast Guard rescue boat pulls alongside two sailors who have abandoned their sinking landing craft. They are wearing full life vests, rather than the life belts used by Army personnel. A line goes to the sailor nearest the boat, and the second sailor holds his breath as he awaits his turn. The man at far right waits with rope in hand to throw out to the second sailor.

RESCUE AND EVACUATION OF CASUALTIES

Throughout the day, rescue and evacuation missions kept pace with the actions. The sixty Coast Guard cutters that had been converted to rescue ships proved their worth many times over (5-57 and 5-58). Serious casualties were evacuated to England as rapidly as possible (5-59 and 5-60). These missions of mercy were by no means exempt from the horrors of war.

With most of the 16th Regiment's medical corps embarked for landing at Fox Green, Omaha Beach, *LCI-85* became lodged on a beach obstacle. A shell struck the LCI, setting it afire and destroying the gangway. The skipper, Lt. (jg) Coit Handley, USCGR (U.S. Coast Guard Reserve), managed to back the craft out from the beach and put out the fires. At 1100 he was directed to nurse his stricken craft back to *Samuel Chase*, where he was able to transfer his casualties before the LCI went down (5-61). Other vessels were

5-58. The second of the two sailors comes aboard. Note the belt securing the rescuer to the boat.

5-59. An LCM littered with debris evacuates casualties to a larger vessel. The seriously wounded are being loaded onto a platform that will be raised onto the deck of the transport.

5-60. The crew hoists the platform with casualties from the LCM on board the transport. These are among the first casualties to be evacuated on 6 June. Empty Navy litters in the foreground await the wounded.

5-61. *LCI-85*, struck by German shell fire, comes close aboard *Samuel Chase* to off-load casualties.

5-62. Casualties from the invasion on board an LST hospital ship are transported back to England. Stretcher-borne casualties await assignment to a bunk.

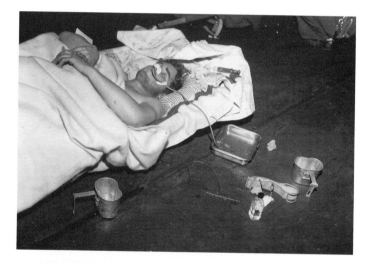

fortunate enough to transport their wounded safely back to England (5-62, 5-63, and 5-64).

AIRBORNE DIVISION ACTIVITY

From the first, using Airborne troops was controversial. The ground commanders had asked that Airborne troops be dropped behind Utah before the beach landings to cut off any German counterattack and to clear the way for the Americans to advance toward Cherbourg. Air Chief Marshall Leigh-Mallory was sure this tactic would fail and estimated casualties would be a totally unacceptable figure. Bradley countered that without this move he could not order the Utah landings. After considering all sides, Eisenhower agreed to use Airborne troops.

The force crossed the Channel without incident. But once over France, it looked like Leigh-Mallory's gloomy predictions would come true. The planes encountered heavy German AA fire; the weather was foggy and cloudy; several drops were scattered. The aircraft either sent off the troops too soon or overshot the drop sites. A few men of the British 6th Airborne landed smack on the lawn of the German

5-63. A seriously wounded serviceman sleeps while a tube drains fluid from his nose into a basin on the deck.

5-64. A buttock wound forces this glum serviceman to rest on his stomach. Note the piping along the bulkhead of the LST.

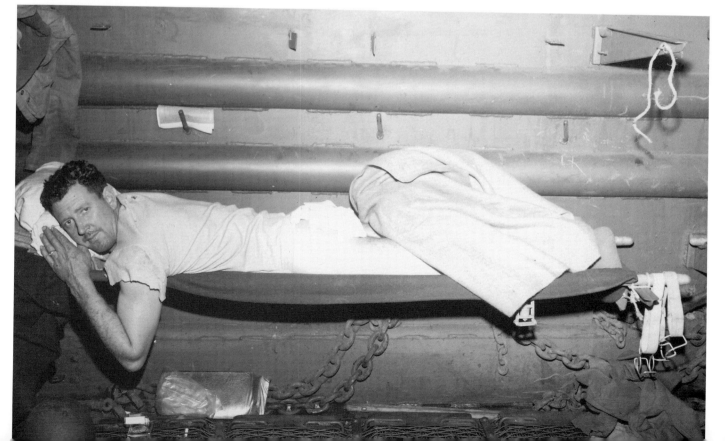

716th Infantry Division Headquarters and were promptly captured. Many men of the U.S. 82d and 101st Airborne divisions fell into the inundated fields and swamps and drowned. The hedgerows separated units so that regrouping took most of the night. Two regiments of the 82d were thus scattered, and at the end of D-Day some four thousand of the 101st Division's sixty-six hundred men lacked unified control.

Nevertheless, these Airborne troops knew the meaning of initiative. The scattered men formed themselves into platoons or squads and set to work cutting telephone wires, shooting or capturing German messengers, and in general frustrating small enemy units. Some well-dropped units of the 82d managed to capture the town of Ste.-Mère-Église by 0430 (5-65). This and the following photos taken at Ste.-Mère-Église give no hint of the hardships just encountered. In spite of the tragic losses, casualties were far behind Leigh-Mallory's estimate, and as the gentleman he was, Leigh-Mallory congratulated Eisenhower on the wisdom of his decision.

Most of the following group of photos seem to have been taken at Ste.-Mère-Église between 7 and 10 June, and they give a fairly representative picture of a Normandy town following the Allied landings. Here are shops and buildings, including a construction materials concern and the office of a newspaper, *Le Petit Journal* (5-66). Taken on 7 June, about half a block down toward the newspaper office, photo 5-67 shows two members of the 82d Airborne patrolling the streets.

5-65. Four Americans of the 82d Airborne Division enter Ste.-Mère-Église in the early morning shadows of 6 June. The sergeant at left is armed with a Thompson submachine gun, Model M-1 with a 30-round box magazine. These simplified weapons differed from the M1928 version in that they would not accept the large drum magazine so often associated with the gangster era of the 1920s and 1930s. Also the front handle was replaced by a simple wooden grip.

5-67. Two mounted members of the 82d Airborne patrol the streets of Ste.-Mère-Église on 7 June.

5-66. A deserted street in Ste.-Mère-Eglise following the 82d Airborne assault, 10 June.

5-68. Two French refugees try to communicate with an American paratrooper.

5-69. Clutching their belongings, the same two refugees at right center press on through the village.

In photo **5-68**, two Frenchwomen, probably mother and daughter, are talking—or trying to talk—to a paratrooper, who predictably is devoting his attention to the attractive younger woman. Evidently the trio managed to understand one another, for in photo **5-69** the women are proceeding on their way. The building at right is where they were talking. The store at far left run by M. Lemenicier appears to be Ste.-Mère-Église's one-stop shopping market, as it does triple duty as a gas station, grocery (*épicerie*), and hardware store (*quincaillerie*).

5-70. A member of the 82d Airborne assists two refugees who return with their belongings to Ste.-Mère-Église on 8 June.

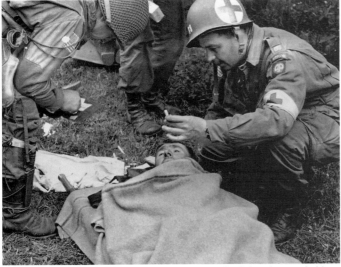

5-71. A captain of one of the 82d Airborne's medical detachments holds a cigarette for a comrade wounded during the fighting on 6–7 June. The man at left is probably taking down information regarding the wounded man.

5-72. Dead German paratroopers from Oberst von der Heydte's 6th Fallschirmjäger Regiment are lined up and arranged for burial.

5-73. C-47s of the IX Transport Command tow in gliders past troops fighting on Utah Beach, near Les Dunes de Madeleine.

By 8 June, some residents must have considered it safe to return, for photo **5-70** shows two other refugees, loaded with blankets, packages, a suitcase, and coat hangers, returning to Ste.-Mère-Église. Two sobering scenes—one of a wounded American (**5-71**), the other of dead Germans (**5-72**)—end this group of photos. French civilians nearby seem more concerned with salvaging the silk from an American parachute than with these enemy corpses. After all, one must be practical!

Of course, the Airborne troops would need personnel and equipment reinforcements, and this was planned for the evening of 6 June. Photo **5-73** depicts part of the effort to supply the 82d and 101st Airborne divisions several miles behind Utah Beach. Senior officers naturally followed progress with the keenest interest (**5-74**).

5-74. Brigadier General Gavin, the 82d Airborne's bridgehead commander and assistant commander of the division, studies a map of Normandy with his chief of staff, Maj. Wilherd E. Harrison (right).

5-75. A Ninth Air Force B-26 Marauder returning to England on 6 June. This photo was taken near Lion-sur-Mer, Sword Beach, in the British landing area. Note LCTs unloading below and the bewildering patchwork quilt of the *bocage* behind the beaches.

OTHER AIR ACTIVITY

The weather that, though not ideal, was good enough for naval and ground action, seriously hampered the planned air support. Over eight hundred medium bombers—A-20s and B-26s of the Ninth Air Force—bombed coastal defenses and transportation targets (5-75). The Eighth Air Force flew four missions on 6 June in support of the invasion (5-76). At Omaha Beach, to avoid the possibility of hitting the landing craft, the bombardiers were ordered to delay their drops for 30 seconds. As a result, their bombs fell several miles beyond the beach, destroying crops and killing cattle. The second mission, targeting transportation centers, encountered complete cloud cover, and most of the 528 heavy bombers returned to England with their loads still in place. The third and fourth missions also targeted key transportation positions. A measure of the poor German resistance is the fact that the Eighth Air Force lost only three aircraft—to ground fire and a collision. Results, however, were disappointing. In fact, some action reports give the impression that nobody could see anything, and any strikes on valuable targets were pure luck.

Both the Eighth and Ninth Air Forces provided fighters for escort, ground support, and dive-bombing. The two forces pooled their P-38 Lightnings to provide cover for the convoys steaming back and forth across the English Channel. Royal Air Force (RAF) Fighter Command provided low cover over the beaches, while the U.S. IX Fighter Command provided high cover. The 354th was the Ninth Air Force's first fighter unit and had brought its Mustangs over to En-

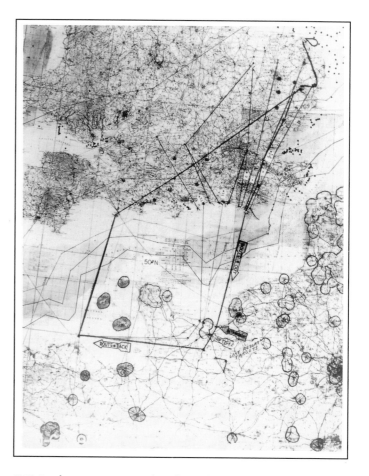

5-76. Bomb group routing map from the Ninth Air Force on 6 June 1944. Note the path from the English airfields to Normandy and the "last resort" target identified.

5-77. The IX Fighter Command P-51C Mustangs of the 354th Fighter Group pull up and away from their airfields in England during 6 June.

gland in November 1943 (5-77).

The American covering operations were incredibly uneventful, so successful had been the pre-invasion bombing campaign against the Luftwaffe. Only three FW-190 German fighters appeared over the invasion during the day of 6 June. After nightfall, twenty-two German aircraft attacked the invasion fleet, but that was a far cry from what Göring and the Luftwaffe had promised in the event of an invasion. The greatest amphibious operation in history would go forward without a challenge from the German Air Force. One American fighter pilot, disappointed with the lack of targets, exclaimed in disgust, "The *Luftwaffe* had leftwaffe." General Arnold's words, "Where was the *Luftwaffe*?" in his book, *Global Mission,* no doubt were on the lips of many in the Wehrmacht during the Normandy campaign.

General Galland, general of the German fighters, calculated after the war that if all the Luftwaffe aircraft available in Normandy had been in the air on 6 June, they still would have been outnumbered twenty-one to one. Those reserves that were brought forward from the Reich's Home Defense units were consumed in the "kiln of the invasion." The bulk of the German fighter forces had to be deployed in a crowded area north of Paris, which meant that they could only attack the invasion force from its flank and that Allied fighter patrols could detect them more easily.

Even with the paucity of aerial targets, American heroism abounded in the skies over Normandy. In photo **5-78** Lieutenant General Brereton, commanding the Ninth Air Force, awards the Silver Star to Capt. Don Beerbower. To Beerbower's right are Brigadier General McCalley and Colonel Bickel, Beerbower's group commander.

5-78. Capt. Don Beerbower *(second from left)* is awarded the Silver Star for action in the skies over Normandy.

5-79. Ninth Air Force fighter pilot 2d Lt. Robert E. Kelso, of Jackson, Michigan, mounts his P-47D Thunderbolt during the early days of the invasion.

5-80. U.S. naval aviators of Cruiser Scouting Squadron 7 (VCS-7) are briefed before flying gun-spotting missions over the Normandy beachheads. Reading *(left to right):* unidentified; Wing Comdr. Robert J. Hardiman, RAF, commanding Allied spotting pilots; Ens. Robert J. Adams, USNR; Maj. Noel East, British Army Intelligence; Lt. Harris Hammersmith, Jr., USNR; Capt. John Ruscoe, Royal Artillery, gunnery liaison officer.

In photo **5-79**, another Ninth Air Force fighter pilot, 2d Lt. Robert E. Kelso, poses with his aircraft. The marking on its wing, well worn on the leading edges, is an invasion stripe. The object of such stripes was to prevent friend-or-foe confusion. As so few German aircraft were to be found, however, the confusion factor was nil.

One of the intriguing facets of aerial activity over Normandy was the use of U.S. Navy pilots flying RAF Mark Vb Spitfire fighter aircraft to perform gun-spotting duty over the beaches (**5-80**). These Navy pilots were drawn from the observation and scouting squadrons of the following ships: heavy cruisers *Augusta*, *Tuscaloosa*, and *Quincy* and battleships *Arkansas*, *Texas*, and *Nevada*. They formed one of the shortest-lived naval squadrons in wartime history—VCS-7.

Though the Mark Vb was obsolete, it was judged sufficient for spotting purposes. The additional speed enjoyed by the Spitfires over the American battleship and cruiser aircraft (OS2U Kingfishers and SOC Seagulls) would enable the Navy men to have some sort of a chance for survival should the Luftwaffe show up in force. Already instructed in aerial spotting, the Americans had only to move over to the Spitfires. In that regard, they were instructed, ironically, by

other Americans, USAAF pilots of the 6th Observation Group.

The pace of the spotting efforts was hectic—one Spitfire was lost to flak on 6 June, and others were attacked by Luftwaffe fighters the next day. VCS-7 continued service through the Cherbourg operation. When Cherbourg fell, the squadron was disbanded after 209 sorties and 8 combat losses.

In photo **5-81**, we see one of the aircraft the Navy left in England, and in **5-82**, two naval aviators, Lt. (jg) Robert F. Doyle and Ens. John F. Mudge, congratulate one another on their safe return to England. Both had distinguished themselves. Doyle was awarded the Air Medal for his "fearless determination and remain[ing] constantly over dangerous areas until all targets were effectively neutralized or destroyed. . . ." Mudge likewise received the Air Medal for "his skill and courage in the face of heavy anti-aircraft fire . . . provid[ing] accurate spotting for naval gunfire."

A day like no other, 6 June 1944 passed into history. No one who lived through it would ever forget it, although many wished that they could.

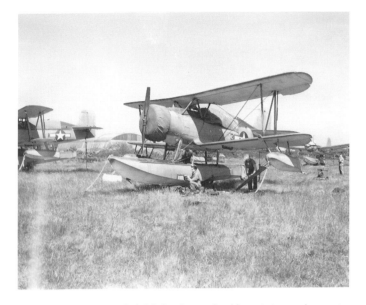

5-81. Curtiss SOC Seagulls left behind in England by U.S. Navy observation pilots. Maintenance men service aircraft to keep the machines ready for action. A lone Vought OS2U Kingfisher lies at far right in the distance.

5-82. Lt. (jg) Robert F. Doyle shakes hands with his wingman, Ens. John F. Mudge, after their return from a gun-spotting and strafing mission.

CHAPTER 6

Allied Buildup and Consolidation: 7 June–15 June

7 JUNE

Ancon, the amphibious force flagship, was well fitted out as a floating headquarters (6-1) with special facilities for intelligence, communications, plotting, and planning. This photo of the Joint Operations Room was taken during the invasion of Sicily, but no doubt it looked much the same for the Normandy operation (6-2). Despite these excellent facilities, Major General Gerow quickly left the Ancon to establish V Corps headquarters on the beach, setting out at about 2000 on 6 June. Roughly an hour earlier, Major General Huebner had set up 1st Division headquarters on shore.

At this point, the high command had three main objectives: first, to follow through quickly with the buildup; second, to expand at Caen, to which the Germans assigned great importance; and third and most urgent, to consolidate the beachheads into a single, strong line. To that end, Eisenhower decided to visit Normandy with Admiral Ramsay on 7 June to confer with Montgomery and Bradley (6-3).

Bradley and Rear Admiral Hall awaited Ike's arrival on Augusta, anchored in berth L-12 off Omaha Beach. In addition to Ramsay's flag, Apollo, which brought the visiting party from England, flew a red flag with four stars for the

6-1. Two patrol craft maneuver off the starboard beam of *Ancon* while standing by off Omaha Beach during the landings of 7 June.

supreme commander. After this meeting, Eisenhower met with Montgomery near Arromanches and toured the invasion beaches.

Returning to Great Britain, Ike asked *Apollo*'s skipper to steam close to shore opposite the British sector so that he could see the British beaches more clearly. *Apollo* ran aground on a three-fathom "patch," or sandbar, damaging its propellers and drive shaft. Eisenhower and Ramsay transferred to the destroyer HMS *Undaunted* for the remainder of the voyage to Portsmouth, making port about 2200. Typically, he was concerned lest the *Apollo*'s captain be punished for something that he, Eisenhower, considered to be his own fault. Ramsay assured him that although an inquiry was inevitable, the captain probably would suffer nothing worse than a reprimand.

6-2. Joint Operations Room on board *Ancon*. The message on the blackboard at right reads, "Again we have been asked to do the impossible. Let's do it as usual."

6-3. A pensive General Eisenhower sips a cup of coffee somewhere in the English Channel off the coast of France, probably aboard the minelayer HMS *Apollo*.

6-4. "You name it, boss, we'll hit it." Crews on the battleship *Arkansas* deliver a message to their skipper, Capt. Frederick G. Richards. Note details of range finder at right. At left on the forecastle, crewmen limber up with a medicine ball.

6-5. One of the invasion beaches photographed from a Ninth Air Force reconnaissance aircraft.

During the buildup and consolidation on 7 June, the Navy continued to support the ground troops with salvos of largely accurate gunfire (**6-4**). Photo **6-5** shows *Arkansas* and its companions in the bombardment forces have hit their target on Omaha. The beach areas are pockmarked with craters and strewn with still-burning targets. As the invasion progressed, the ships' fire was directed farther and farther inland, increasing the need for the VCS-7 Spitfire spotting pilots.

The Eighth Air Force's heavy bombers doggedly tried to keep enemy reinforcements from moving up, but once again heavy cloud cover proved troublesome. Almost one hundred bombers were unable to bomb their targets. The Eighth's fighters met some 150 German aircraft, destroying 31. After approximately two thousand sorties, some twenty-five U.S. fighters were lost.

The Ninth Air Force sent over six hundred medium bombers to hit transportation and coastal ranges. Its aerial reconnaissance duties continued, as seen in photo **6-6**.

Meanwhile, buildup on the beaches went forward unabated (**6-7**). At Omaha, troop and equipment landings

6-6. Another reconnaissance aircraft photographs a German motorized column struggling to move up to the Normandy front.

6-7. An aerial shot of the vehicles (tanks or DUKWs) coming ashore, the men clustered on the beach, and the landing craft at center.

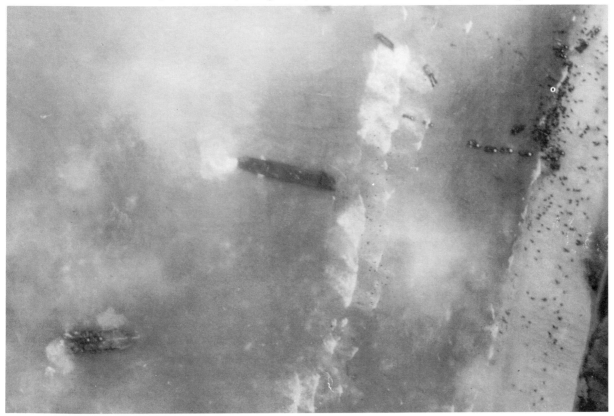

6-8. An improvised wire-mesh road provides a thoroughfare for supplies moving up. Note the rocky, gravelly nature of the ground and the markers for the beach.

were still behind schedule, but the situation was improving with matériel reaching frontline troops (6-8). The 29th Division drove forward with the double objective of joining with the VII Corps at Utah Beach and of relieving the Rangers at Pointe du Hoc (6-9).

The Navy support forces suffered more casualties, among them the minesweeper *Tide*. On the morning of 7 June, *Tide* swept the area between St.-Marcouf and Barfleur, clearing lanes for fire support ships. The sweeper drifted over Cardonnet Banks, exploded a mine, and sank while under tow (6-10).

Elements of the 101st Airborne were bogged down near Carentan, a small village lying between two soggy marshlands. Others found the going easier. In photo 6-11, members of the 101st have just rounded up a group of German prisoners and are making friends in Ste.-Marie-du-Mont. The 101st patches are clearly visible although, as mentioned, this was forbidden.

6-9. A French peasant gives information to a corporal of the 29th Division during the push inland on 7 June near Vierville-sur-Mer. The two soldiers at left are armed with an M-1 carbine and Thompson submachine gun.

6-10. Minesweeper USS *Tide* (AM-125) burns after striking a mine near the invasion beaches. *PT-509* (*at left*) and *Pheasant* (AM-61) at right stand by *Tide*, which lies at center.

6-11. Members of the 101st Airborne Division charm the locals in Ste.-Marie-du-Mont. All the young girls are at the center of attention.

6-12. C-47s of the IX Transport Command fly low over Utah Beach during the effort to resupply troops of the 82d and 101st Airborne divisions. Another group of C-47s is at lower left.

6-13. C-47s of the Troop Carrier Command, Ninth Air Force, tow gliders over the bomb-pocked shores.

6-14. Ninth Air Force gliders clutter fields during Airborne landings in support of the Normandy invasion. Sherman tanks are on the road in the middle distance, and C-47s circle overhead.

6-15. Swooping down low, a C-47 prepares to drop out supplies to the Americans waiting below. Parachutes from the previous drop appear at top.

Resupply of the 101st and 82d—a portion of which was isolated on the Merderet River—posed a special problem. The Twelfth Air Force responded with over four hundred C-47s, C-53s, and gliders. Naturally this spectacular mission provided not only supplies to the paratroopers but a bonanza of photographic opportunities, as evidenced by the following series of photos (**6-12** through **6-20**).

6-16. A C-47 dropping supplies and equipment.

6-17. Parachutes blossom, no doubt to the great relief of those on the ground.

6-18. Airborne personnel below scurry to retrieve supplies left behind in the parachute drop.

6-19. Roaring past the cameraman at low altitude, a C-47 picks up a Waco glider in Normandy.

6-20. Troops of the 101st Airborne receive directions from Military Police (MPs) stationed at a crossroads. The gliders in the background are of the British Airspeed "Horsa" type.

Supply and reinforcement efforts were fraught with danger. The small fields and hedgerows made glider activity exceptionally hazardous; accidents were inevitable. The glider shown in photo **6-21** probably was used by the 327th Glider Infantry Regiment of the 101st. Other evidence of tragedy appears in photos **6-22** and **6-23**.

6-21. A wrecked American glider that crashed in an orchard near Ste.-Marie-du-Mont on 7 June. Note the invasion stripes on the wings and serial number visible on the tail.

6-22. Dead American soldiers lie near their glider. A gas can and rations ("Field Ration K—Breakfast Unit") are also strewn about.

6-23. Crash-landed Allied glider near Hiesville, about four miles southeast of Ste.-Mère-Église, on 7 June.

8 JUNE

By the night of 7–8 June, the German high command evidently had begun to take the invasion of Normandy seriously, and had set major forces out to repel it. U.S. and British air power must concentrate on slowing down these enemy reinforcements. All other strategic, tactical, and even humanitarian considerations must be set aside. In the ensuing raids of that night and throughout the day, not only valuable targets but inevitably towns and farms were smashed.

The Eighth Air Force had to abort about 400 heavy bomber assignments due to cloud cover, but 735 went on to attack airfields, bridges, other transportation and communication targets, and the usual targets of opportunity. Three of these bombers were lost. Meanwhile the Eighth Air Force fighters and fighter-bombers flew 1,405 sorties against similar objectives—airfields, troop concentrations, and towns. They claimed destruction of nearly 400 enemy vehicles and 46 aircraft at a cost of 22 fighters lost. The Ninth Air Force sent up some 400 medium bombers against bridges, ammunition dumps, and troops, while some 1,400 fighters supported the medium bombers, provided high cover over the assault area, and bombed and strafed targets similar to the bombers. All this blitzing did slow down the German troop movements but did not stop them.

On the ground, the V Corps moved into Caumont, but in general advances were slow. The 82d kept control of Ste.-Mère-Église. The 29th Division captured Isigny, of Camem-

6-24. Elements of the 101st Airborne press toward the village of St.-Marcouf during 8 June.

bert cheese fame, and headed for Carentan, while men of the 101st moved eastward from the Carentan Canal. Everywhere the Americans encountered strong resistance.

Little of this ground action and none of the fire storm in the skies appear in the following series of photos dealing with the occupation of the town of St.-Marcouf by elements of the 101st Airborne. This took place well behind the front lines and the fighting then under way at St. Côme-du-Mont. In photo **6-24** a peasant chats with an American staff sergeant. Evidently not entirely reassured, a technician 5th grade casts a wary eye to his rear (**6-25**). Paratroopers social-

6-25. With the rest of his squad pressing forward, a technician 5th grade looks to the rear, past the cameraman. The soldiers carry a mix of M-1 carbines and rifles. The soldier at far right advances with a fixed bayonet.

ize with the locals, while other soldiers advance cautiously into the village (**6-26** and **6-27**). Next comes a machine-gun detachment. The 101st has completed the first occupation of a French town, and its members show off the usual "souvenirs" (**6-28, 6-29,** and **6-30**).

At the beaches, 8 June was a busy day. First, during the night of the seventh, ammunition began to run short, so four LCIs were assigned to tow two barges each to the beach for resupply. These barges held 600 tons of explosives apiece. Timing was very precise; the landing had to take place at high tide, which would come at 0100 of the eighth. The Luftwaffe put on a bombing raid at about midnight; but the tide proverbially waits for no man, and at 0045 the LCIs had to move in. Miraculously, all the ships and their barges made it to shore safely.

6-26. Paratroopers mingle with French civilians at St.-Marcouf.

6-27. Soldiers stay near the trees and edge of the road, ready to take advantage of cover if necessary. The village sign has been censored.

6-28. Portions of a machine-gun detachment advance into town. The man at left carries a machine gun, while the man behind him carries a supply of ammunition. The soldier in the background makes ready to come onto the road, perhaps after exploring the rear to the right of the road.

6-29. A detachment from the 101st Airborne Division with a tracked vehicle occupies the first of many French villages and towns to come. Note the soldiers' 101st patches, which the omnipresent censor missed.

6-30. Some 101st Airborne members proudly display their newly won war trophies—a small German national flag and German helmet. Note the hand grenades and all of the equipment the paratroopers carry.

6-31. Troops pouring into the beaches included this detachment of the 5th Engineer Special Brigade, seen here splashing through the surf at Fox Green, Omaha Beach, on 8 June.

6-32. "Yanks everywhere," seen at Red Uncle, Utah Beach, on 8 June. Note the beach identification sign and landing craft in distance. The truck at left prepares to move up the road cut through the dunes. A wire-mesh road has been laid to facilitate traffic moving up and down the beach.

6-33. The destroyer escort USS *Rich* (DE-695) detonates a second mine amidships after losing 50 feet of its stern three minutes before. The ship's 1.1-inch quadruple AA mount aft, just before where the first mine sheared off the stern, is still visible.

Troops and matériel kept coming in (**6-31**) and Omaha was still far behind schedule. In contrast, Utah had no serious congestion of matériel, and seventeen Liberty ships* began landing the 90th Division. Perhaps the scene in photo **6-32** best portrays part of this action. Throughout the day, the Navy continued its invaluable fire support cover.

Of all German weapons, the Allied Navy men participating in Overlord most feared the mines. Even as the ground fighting moved inland, mines claimed vessel after vessel. The DE *Rich* (**6-33**) had gone to assist *Glennon* (DD-840), which had struck a mine, when at 0920 the *Rich* too was stricken. Finally, a third mine sank *Rich* a few minutes later. Of its crew, 27 were killed, 72 wounded, and 62 missing.

Such actions, plus the Germans' counterfire, kept the medics busy (**6-34**). A typical scene of preparations for evacuation appears in photos **6-35** and **6-36**.

*Heavy cargo ships built during WWII for the Merchant Marine.

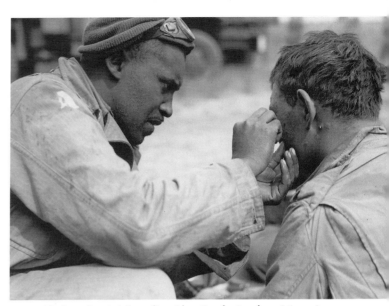

6-34. A black medic administers first aid on Omaha Beach on 8 June. Apparently he is removing bits of shrapnel from the patient's face and neck.

6-35. A casualty being helped aboard an LCVP for evacuation to England clutches a carton of Chesterfield cigarettes. The broad band around the helmets of those assisting designate Navy personnel. A man in the background wades back toward the beach.

6-36. His Chesterfields tucked safely away, the wounded man in the previous photo rests in the landing craft while being transported away from France. Note the Navy men wearing life vests. The wounded soldier immediately in front of the loading ramp has a German helmet as a souvenir, and the man at lower left shields his eyes from the sun.

6-37. Senior U.S. officers watch landing operations from *Augusta*, flagship of Western Naval Task Force, in the morning shadows of 8 June. *Left to right:* Rear Admiral Kirk, commander, Western Naval Task Force; Lieutenant General Bradley, commander, American Ground Forces; unidentified; Capt. Arthur D. Struble, Kirk's chief of staff; and Maj. Gen. Hugh Keen.

6-38. Bradley clambers up a "Jacob's ladder" while coming on board a warship, 8 June, to confer with General Montgomery and Admiral Ramsay, overall commanders of the land and sea operations in Normandy.

6-39. Montgomery climbs on board for the Bradley-Ramsay conference.

6-40. U.S. invasion force commanders inspect Omaha Beach on 8 June. Kirk is at left. Hall, wearing a helmet, is under the beach marker. Bradley stands at right. This was taken at the same location as photo 6-8.

Senior U.S. and British officers kept a close eye on progress at the beaches (6-37). Bradley, his face contorted with determination and possibly pain, climbed stiffly up a "Jacob's ladder" to confer with Ramsay and Montgomery (6-38). Monty, sporting what is likely a regimental badge on his beret, seemed to have less trouble in boarding (6-39). They had a busy day, embarking and disembarking a number of times. In photo 6-40 they are inspecting Omaha Beach. With them are Kirk, in blues, and Hall, wearing his helmet.

Heartening evidence of progress was the completion of an emergency landing strip. Detachments of the "Dozer Devils"—a bulldozer battalion from the IX Aviation Engineer Command, went ashore soon after the landings of 7 June and by the eighth had completed a 2,000-foot emergency landing strip (6-41). A feature of such strips was the "hessian mat," a tar paper–like composition supplied in 200-foot rolls. The matting was rolled out by trucks and cemented into place with a mixture of diesel oil and gasoline expelled by another truck, then rolled like freshly laid asphalt (6-42). In this manner a strip could be completed in less than a day.

Photo 6-43 shows the crew of the first C-47 to land on the beachhead during 8 June. This aircraft functioned as a hospital evacuation craft. And here is the first P-47 to land at the first runway in Normandy (6-44).

6-41. USAAF officers of a bulldozer battalion from the IX Aviation Engineer Command confer during the construction of the Ninth Air Force's emergency landing field near the invasion beaches. *Left to right:* Capt. Raymond N. Carlen and Lt. Col. John J. Livingston talk with Maj. Gen. Ralph Boyce, deputy commander of the Ninth Air Force, and Col. Philip Cole.

6-42. Construction crews lay out hessian mat material on an emergency landing strip just a few miles behind the front lines.

6-43. Crew of an IX Troop Carrier Command C-47—the first such aircraft to land on the beachhead in France during 8 June. Note the crudely painted invasion stripes.

6-44. "Rick O'Shay II," the first P-47 to land on the first runway in Normandy, is armed with a bomb. All Ninth Air Force fighter groups were officially referred to as fighter-bomber groups, reflecting the more diverse mission that would be required in the coming months.

6-45. A DUKW traverses an entry through the dunes at Red Uncle, Utah Beach, on 9 June. Note the beach marker at left. See also photo 4-35.

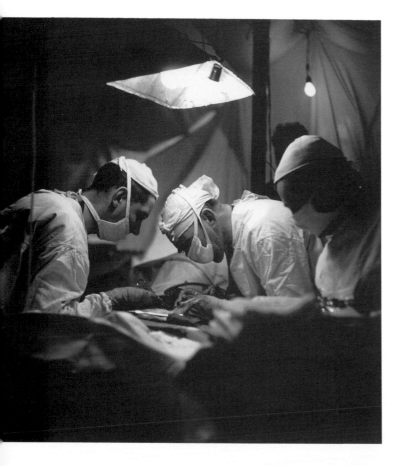

9 JUNE

This day was fairly quiet on the Normandy front. Air activity was practically nil because of bad weather. Only one fighter squadron of the Eighth Air Force attacked shipping, and another flew escort for a photo reconnaissance mission that was not completed. The Eighth lost two of its fighters.

Already the beaches began to take on an orderly look. Wooden sticks had been laid down as a roadbed to assist movement of vehicles and equipment into the areas behind the beaches (6-45). There was time to care for the wounded (6-46), honor the living (6-47), and bury the dead (6-48).

That evening, Hitler came to a decision that may well have ensured the invasion's success. Faced with an Allied campaign in the West and anticipating an invasion from the East, Hitler and Jodl decided to go on the defensive in the West. The führer so advised OB West, ordering him to strengthen the Fifteenth Army at Calais and to stop the Panzer and infantry movements from the Pas-de-Calais to Normandy. Von Rundstedt and Rommel found this order bitterly frustrating.

6-46. Army surgeons work on casualties at a medical clearing station near the beaches during 9 June.

6-47. Distinguished Service Crosses were awarded to leaders of the 101st Airborne on 9 June. *Left to right:* Major General Taylor, division commander; Lt. Col. Patrick F. Cassidy, commanding 1st Battalion, 502d Parachute Infantry Regiment; Capt. Frank L. Lillyman, commander, 101st Airborne Pathfinders; and Chaplain John S. Maloney.

6-48. Armed with an M-1 Thompson submachine gun, a paratrooper of the 101st Airborne stands guard on 9 June over a German burial detail digging graves for their own dead. Taken during the 101st Airborne drive on Carentan, 9 June. The prisoners likely come from the 1058th Grenadier Regiment, 91st Division, taken during the fighting at St. Côme-du-Mont.

6-49. Liberty ship *Charles Morgan* down by the stern off Utah Beach on 10 June. *LST-474* is alongside rendering assistance.

6-50. An LCS (landing craft, support), modified for hydrographic duties, serves as a survey boat on 10 June. Note the survey flag, the stripes on the helmets of the sailors, and a transport lying in the distance.

6-51. A platoon of black troops, armed with rifles and carbines, surround a farmhouse in an effort to clear snipers from the area near Vierville-sur-Mer on 10 June. They are led by Capt. Samuel S. Broussard of Breaux Bridge, Louisiana, shown at the corner of the building. The vertical stripe identifies him as an officer.

10 JUNE

Equally predictable were the reactions of the British and American leaders when on 10 June British Intelligence decoded the German messages. Nevertheless, while Hitler's decision came as a godsend to the Allies, everyone realized that the road ahead would still be long and deadly. Moreover, there was no guarantee that Hitler would not change his mind and concentrate on Normandy.

Weather conditions were still not favorable for heavy bombing runs, but otherwise air activity this day was brisk. Over 200 of the Eighth Air Force's heavy bombers aborted, but 539 got through and attacked airfields and coastal batteries at the cost of one B-24. The VIII Fighter Command flew over 1,600 sorties against the usual communications and tactical targets, claiming 225 German vehicles and 16 German aircraft destroyed while losing 25 fighters. The Ninth Air Force's medium bombers attacked similar targets in the assault area, performed escort duty, and bombed in support of the ground forces.

The waters near the beaches were still hazardous. At 0400 on 10 June, a radio-controlled bomb struck the Liberty ship *Charles Morgan* off Utah Beach, and it went down by the stern. Fortunately, later it was salvaged (**6-49**). Photo **6-50** shows an LCS performing survey duties off the beachheads.

6-52. Captain Broussard climbs down from the ladder after searching the farmhouse.

Mop-up operations were under way, especially targeting German snipers. Fear of these men was very much justified, for they were skillful and clever. They not only held up the American advance but exacted a heavy toll upon any units attempting to move into the interior. The African-American platoon depicted in the following set of photos is flushing out snipers—a difficult, dangerous, and important task (**6-51, 6-52,** and **6-53**).

6-53. The dead German sniper has been picked off by an advancing black assault unit.

11 JUNE

The Eighth Air Force sent up 1,043 heavy bombers, of which over 400 either aborted or failed to bomb for various reasons. The rest hit bridges and airfields on the Brest peninsula and near Paris, as well as coastal defenses in the Pas-de-Calais area. Three were lost. The Ninth Air Force's medium bombers hit targets of the usual type, including, regrettably, "town areas"—a term occurring many times since 8 June.

Though the beachheads became progressively safer, they and the surrounding waters were not immune to German attack. An E-boat torpedoed the fleet tug *Partridge*, which was helping to tow a pontoon runway; *Patridge* sank immediately. A torpedo from the same group of E-boats also hit *LST-528*, but it managed to reach the beach, unload, and after undergoing emergency repairs, get back to business. A German aircraft broke through the RAF's low fighter cover and sprayed the Americans at the beach with bullets (6-54). The same strafing attack caught men on a Rhino ferry unawares, and *LCT-522* had to back away before unloading all of its cargo (6-55).

Photo 6-56 shows one of the U.S. Navy command posts that had been established by 11 June. In photo 6-57, a Navy hospital corpsman takes advantage of a lull in the action to write a V-Mail letter. Readable text says, "I was glad to get another chance to write after so long a time. Right now I'm in France . . . I'll write every chance I get. . . ." Photo 6-58 illustrates these handy V-mail forms.

6-54. Navy beach battalion members dive for cover during a German strafing attack on 11 June. The horizontal helmet band identifies these men as Navy personnel.

6-55. The same strafers attack a Rhino ferry. The man lying on his side at left appears to have been hit.

6-56. U.S. Navy command post on one of the invasion beaches. Note the helmet bands, signal lamp, bull horn, and the heavily sandbagged structure.

6-57. A Navy hospital corpsman takes time to send a letter home, using a V-Mail form.

6-58. V-Mail form provided to Navy servicemen so that they might notify home newspapers or radio stations of their role in the invasion.

No. _____

CENSORS STAMP

Commander U.S.Naval
Forces in Europe.
SENDERS NAME
(Public Relations Section)
SENDERS ADDRESS
Fleet P.O.,New York N.Y.

DATE

Naval Personnel: This letter is to inform your home town newspaper or radio station of your part in the European invasion. Fill in name and location of newspaper or radio station above (use separate sheet if you wish to send to more than one). Then print with ink in the blank spaces below. Do not include the name of your ship nor any information other than that requested.

Note to Editors: The below information has been censored and is for immediate release. Names of ships may not be used unless officially announced by the Navy Department.

I, _____ Age _____ Rank _____
   (first name)   (initial)   (last name)   (spell out)

USN - USNR _____, was a member of a U.S. Naval crew in the American Assault Force which
(cross out one)
invaded _____. This was - was not my first action with the enemy.
        (country)   (cross out one)

I saw previous action at _____. I have received the

following promotion _____. I have received
                    (from)   (to)   (date)

the following medals or citations _____,

My home address is _____.
                   (street and number)   (city)   (county)   (state)

My parents are _____. Their address is _____
                                                      (street and number)

_____. My wife's name is _____
(city)   (county)   (state)

_____
(name and address of nearest relative if unmarried and your parents are not living)

Brothers and sisters in service _____
                                (state branch of service and where serving if known)

My occupation before joining the Navy was _____
                                          (include name and address of employer)

_____. The last school I attended was _____.

V····MAIL

6-59. Prime Minister Churchill journeys to the invasion beaches. He chats with General Brooke on the deck of the destroyer HMS *Kelvin*. Note Churchill's ever-present cigar and the machine gun at center behind the two men.

6-60. General Smuts gazes toward the coast of France during the voyage to Montgomery's headquarters.

6-61. General Montgomery steps off the launch bringing Churchill, Smuts, and Brooke to Montgomery's headquarters.

12 JUNE

In the air, the Eighth Air Force sent up 1,278 bombers, losing eight, mostly to ground fire. A group of these fighters encountered about fifty German fighters, and in the ensuing fierce air battle, eight P-47s and five ME-109s were shot down. The Ninth Air Force's aircraft were also very active against their customary targets.

But the most visible action of 12 June was on the VIP (very important person) front. Montgomery had established his headquarters on 8 June at a chateau near Creully, about fifteen miles east of Omaha. By the tenth, he had felt sufficiently confident to invite Churchill for a visit. Churchill immediately accepted. On the twelfth he arrived aboard the destroyer HMS *Kelvin*. With him was Gen. Sir Alan Brooke, chief of the Imperial General Staff (**6-59**), and Gen. Jan C. Smuts, premier of the Union of South Africa (**6-60**). The "father of South Africa" took no active part in the invasion, but he had been present at a 15 May briefing given by the various commanders to an audience that included King George VI and Churchill. Smuts had also witnessed loading procedures in early June.

Monty was in high spirits as he greeted his visitors (**6-61**), and even the weather cooperated. Churchill was quite satisfied with what he saw and learned. On the way home, *Kelvin* passed near the capital ships so that Churchill could witness the bombardment of German positions. Of course, Churchill asked if Kelvin could "have a plug at them." The admiral in charge agreed. The destroyer fired off a salvo, then beat a hasty retreat, for it had come within range of the German guns.

The American top brass paid a concurrent visit to the American sectors. Chief of Staff General Marshall, Chief of Naval Operations Admiral King, and General Hap Arnold, USAAF—all were in England for high-level decision-making—accompanied Eisenhower to Normandy. They traveled with Churchill's party to Portsmouth, where the group split up, and the Americans boarded the USS *Thompson*. They disembarked at Omaha Beach (**6-62** and **6-63**).

6-62. American Army and Navy Chiefs pay their first visit to the beachheads of France on 12 June. Rear Admiral Kirk disembarks *(at left)* from the DUKW, followed by Generals Marshall, Arnold, and Eisenhower.

6-63. The "Big Brass" in Normandy *(left to right):* General Arnold, Admiral King, General Eisenhower, and General Marshall. One wonders what has their attention at right.

6-64. M-4 Sherman tank "Cannon Ball" lies mired on Omaha Beach, 12 June.

They lunched on K rations at First Army Headquarters near Pointe du Hoc, where Gerow and Bradley briefed them. As they toured the area in jeeps, the troops recognized Eisenhower and cheered him.

Landings continued on 12 June, with some difficulty. As noted, a failure of the Normandy campaign was the small number of armored vehicles that landed successfully on 6 June. Now, six days later, an M-4 Sherman tank was mired at Omaha Beach (**6-64**). An Army truck was more successful. A breathing tube had been installed to enable the vehicle to splash ashore without flooding out the engine (**6-65**).

Tides were a major consideration when determining a time to land successfully. On 12 June low tides stranded a pontoon causeway (**6-66**) and *LST-325* (**6-67**). This was a dangerous situation, because its bow hanging so high placed considerable strain on the ship's keel and hull.

After their K rations lunch, the American VIPs learned that a battle was in progress at Carentan. First they heard that the 101st Airborne had taken the town, then that a major German counterattack was under way. However, the 101st prevailed. The Airborne troops shown in photo **6-68** probably are men of the 101st's 2d Battalion, 506th Regiment, heading west through the intersection of the roads to Cherbourg and Paris.

Although it had no immediate effect on the Normandy front, a new and sinister phase of the war opened on 12 June, when the first German V-1 rockets hit Brighton, Kent, and London. Damage was minor, and many shrugged off the attack—an attitude that would soon change perforce.

6-65. An Army Dodge 4 x 4, 3/4-ton truck, nicknamed "Sadie," comes ashore on Utah Beach during the 12 June landings. The stenciling on the front bumper has been censored, but the truck likely carries troops of the 90th Infantry Division.

6-66. Low tide leaves a pontoon causeway (see 6-92) high and dry on 12 June. Note the breakwater of sunken vessels on the horizon.

6-67. With *LST-325* stranded at low tide, workmen construct a sand ramp at left to permit unloading.

6-68. Troops of the 101st Airborne push forward on 12 June through Carentan, the first French town taken by the Allied armies in Normandy. Note the highway signs on the restaurant on the corner. The jeep at left tows an antitank gun.

6-69. Destroyer USS *Nelson* (DD-623) in dry dock at Portsmouth, England, showing torpedo damage sustained on 13 June.

6-70. *Nelson* proceeds toward Boston under tow on 26 August following temporary repairs at Londonderry, Northern Ireland. Towline extends from the bow.

6-71. 1st Lt. Merle Kirstein from Des Moines, Iowa, uses a metal detector to ferret out any antipersonnel mines that may still lie buried in a minefield. Note the German *Minen* sign and the mines awaiting disposal.

13 JUNE

The prospect of nightly German E-boat sorties from Cherbourg and subsequent attacks still troubled the ships posted near the invasion beaches, particularly at night. The destroyer *Nelson* was part of the antisubmarine and E-boat screen near the Omaha beachhead. Anchored in position during the night of 12 June, it made radar contact with an approaching group of German E-boats. *Nelson* fired ten salvos at the intruders, then a torpedo struck *Nelson*, blowing off its stern. Twenty-four men died or were missing, and nine wounded. After emergency repairs, *Nelson* steamed to Boston and was fitted with a new stern (6-69 and 6-70).

Cloud cover was less than anticipated on 13 June, so the Eighth Air Force's heavy bombers flew successful missions over northern France, losing two B-24s. Their fighters claimed to have downed six German aircraft and destroyed many ground vehicles, at a loss of four fighters. The Ninth Air Force struck the usual assortment of rail and road junctions and other logistics and tactical targets.

Mines presented an ongoing problem. Photo 6-71 pictures a lieutenant searching for antipersonnel mines, using a metal detector. Evacuation missions continued for both the American wounded and the German prisoners of war. A view from an LST shows both types—American casualties rest on stretchers on the back of a jeep, while POWs file by in the distance (6-72). In photo 6-73, stretcher-bearers move a wounded man aboard an LST.

6-72. Seen from an American LST, evacuations—American wounded and POWs—are under way.

6-73. Stretcher bearers take the first of two wounded servicemen onto a waiting LST. This photo was apparently taken at very low tide. Note the dozer behind the jeep.

6-74. Destroyer HMS *Scorpion*, which bore visiting Admiral Stark, commander, U.S. Naval Forces, Europe, across the English Channel on his inspection tour of the invasion beaches on 14 June. This picture was taken just before Stark boarded.

6-75. Admiral Stark and Rear Admiral Kirk on board *Scorpion* en route to Normandy. Kirk's short zip-up jacket makes him easy to identify in a large number of photos.

14 JUNE

As mid-month approached, the Eighth Air Force's targets moved farther and farther inland. The Eighth conducted sorties against strategic targets in Germany as well as tactical objectives in France, some southwest of Paris.

VIPs continued to inspect the beaches. Gen. Charles de Gaulle visited the area on 14 June. A less prickly caller that same day was Admiral Stark, who came over from England aboard the British destroyer HMS *Scorpion* (6-74). Stark's white hair and kindly expression reminded everybody of their favorite grandfather. As commander of naval forces in Europe, he was not directly involved with Overlord, but as a former CNO he still exerted considerable influence (6-75). Certainly the photographers took full advantage of the opportunity to snap this popular figure while he toured the invasion beaches with Admiral Kirk (6-76, 6-77, and 6-78).

Of course, there were plenty of ordinary scenes to record, such as aircraft parked (6-79) or, regrettably, crashed (6-80). And the flow of troops and equipment continued unabated (6-81, 6-82, and 6-83).

6-76. Rear Admiral Kirk boards *Augusta* (CA-31) during Stark's visit to Normandy. Note the heavy cruiser's graded camouflage, rivet heads on the side of the ship, and the boarding ladder.

6-77. *PT-199* chops its way through the waters off Normandy, speeding Admiral Stark and his party toward their destination. Note British hospital ship at left.

6-78. Admiral Stark on his inspection tour of the beaches; Rear Admiral Kirk sits in the back seat. The two other officers are unidentified.

6-79. Scene at Omaha Beach on 14 June at a newly constructed airfield overlooking the beach near St. Laurent. A P-38J or L with invasion stripes, likely being employed in convoy cover, lies parked on the very end of the runway.

6-80. On 14 June, a forlorn P-47D rests on an invasion beach where it crash-landed during the early phases of the landings. The site is probably Utah Beach, as there are no high bluffs or cliffs behind the beach in the background.

6-81. A flood of men and vehicles continues to pour into Omaha Beach. Note the DUKW at right, the jeep and trailer at center, the grading equipment at left, and a barrage balloon still floating above the beach.

6-82. Another 50 yards down the road lies a clearing station and information station. (See previous photo, *left center.*) The influx was presumably the 2d Division, whose lead elements disembarked on 12 June.

6-83. Transports and landing craft off Omaha Beach, 14 June. A nest of LCMs lies moored to the transport at right. Note the LCVP at left and its smaller comparative size to the LCMs, which were designed to land vehicles.

15 JUNE

By this time, the V Corps had advanced beyond the range of naval fire support; the Eighth Air Force pounded oil refineries in Germany and tactical targets in France; and the Ninth Air Force concentrated on German fuel and ammunition dumps and communications facilities. In England, thirteen V-1 rockets fell, dispelling any notion that this weapon was just a gimmick. Operation Crossbow—the bombing of V-1 launch sites—would have to step up, even if it meant diverting bombers from strategical and tactical targets in Germany and France.

Mines continued to take their toll. *LST-133* struck one and went down by the stern (6-84), but this ship survived the apparently fatal damage and later took part in the invasion of Okinawa. Even the Bikini atomic test could not finish off *LST-133*. Eventually, on 11 May 1948, it was sunk as a target.

Eisenhower scheduled a visit to the British sector, taking along his son John, who had just graduated from West Point. Montgomery had left his headquarters, so the Eisenhower party visited the area of Bayeux, which had experienced little damage. John noted with surprise that the French people seemed less than enthusiastic about the Allied invasion, downright sullen, in fact. From the Norman point of view, this was not astonishing. Needing Normandy's produce, the Germans had treated the area reasonably well, and the locals had enjoyed a measure of prosperity. Perhaps the arrival of the British and Americans meant the eventual recovery of France, but in the meantime it meant dead countrymen, bombed-out towns, and ruined farms. So one wonders what feelings really animated the Norman who attempted to communicate with such soldiers as PFC Rocco Festa, earnestly striving to learn a bit of French (6-85).

Where troops go, nurses are not far behind. Here 2d Lt. Paula Krull looks over an injury to Chaplain John J. Donovan's left index finger inflicted by a sniper's bullet (6-86).

6-84. *LST-133* down by the stern and beached off Normandy on 15 June, after striking a German mine.

6-86. Chaplain John H. Donovan, attached to the First Army's 51st Field Hospital, chats with 2d Lt. Paula Krull on Omaha Beach, 15 June. She was one of the first frontline nurses to arrive in Normandy.

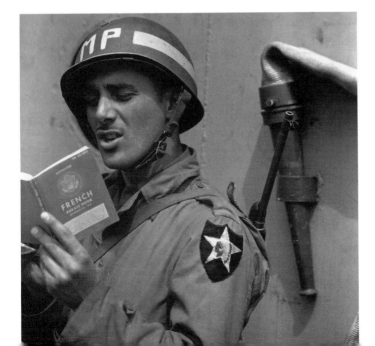

6-85. PFC Rocco Festa, of the 2d Division's Headquarters and Military Police Company, tries his hand at French as he awaits transfer to a landing craft on 15 June. This was no idle diversion, for an MP's contact with the civilian population would be considerable.

6-87. Panorama of a Navy beach master unit during the postinvasion buildup, 15 June 1944.

6-89. Panoramic view of Omaha Beach around mid-June.

6-88. U.S. small craft recovery and repair unit on 15 June.

This period must have seemed an auspicious moment for unit pictures. When the photographer pivoted to record the right-hand side of the sandbagged structure with a second exposure, many of the men moved over to get into the second shot (6-87).

Through hard use, equipment was bound to break down sooner or later. The small craft recovery and repair unit pictured in photo 6-88 had been in operation since D-Day.

Photo 6-89 shows how Omaha Beach looked around 15 June. Bulldozing is in progress at the far left, barrage balloons are in the sky, and a landing craft and equipment are stockpiled at various points. The house near the beach at the center still stands, although damaged heavily by shell fire. In a subsequent photo of this same area, the house has been bulldozed and removed. Note the breakwater formed by the line of sunken merchant vessels in the distance.

ARTIFICIAL HARBOR FACILITIES

The military landings at Normandy involved a tremendous engineering effort. Owing to the unprotected nature of the Norman coast in the vicinity of the invasion beaches, artificial harbor facilities, or Mulberries, were constructed. The main components for these harbors were the floating docks and Rhino causeways (to provide the physical link between incoming shipping and the beach) and the breakwaters that would actually create the sheltered, artificial harbor. Just how useful the Mulberries actually were is debatable. Some believe they were not worth the material and effort that went into them; others believed their value was critical.

DOCKS AND CAUSEWAY

By mid-month, the process for off-loading vehicles had evolved into a several-staged operation. First, usually, the LST that had transported the vehicle from England would deposit it onto a small landing craft, such as an LCM (**6-90**). Next the LCM, which was more adept at approaching the beaches, unloaded its cargo onto a causeway composed of Rhino ferries (**6-91**). The Rhino causeway comprised the last half mile or so of the voyage into the beach. Note that the head of the dock pictured in **6-92** can handle traffic simultaneously from three landing craft. The Rhino causeway terminated on the beach itself (**6-93** and **6-94**).

6-90. A jeep rolls out of *LST-282* onto an LCT during its transfer to the invasion beaches 15 June.

6-91. Army truck lumbers off an LCM onto a Rhino causeway. Note the man at left perched on a bollard.

6-92. Vehicles proceed down the Rhino causeway toward Omaha Beach.

6-93. Black Seabees labor to secure wire-mesh roadway material onto the sands of Omaha Beach.

6-94. An American M-3 half-track leads a column of vehicles about to exit the causeway onto Omaha Beach, completing its transfer from England to France.

6-95. After its construction in Portsmouth, England, a Phoenix caisson with an AA mount is towed into position across from one of the British invasion beaches.

PHOENIX CAISSONS-BREAKWATER

These concrete caissons, 200 feet in length and varying in tonnage, were towed across the channel and sunk end to end to form breakwaters perpendicular to the beaches. The American and British beaches required a total of six miles of these caissons (**6-95, 6-96,** and **6-97**).

6-96. U.S. Army tugs coax a Phoenix caisson across the English Channel for placement in one of the artificial harbors off Normandy.

6-97. Caissons placed in position and sunk as part of the breakwater for the Mulberry artificial harbors.

6-98. An American Liberty ship stands ready to be scuttled and become a portion of an artificial Gooseberry breakwater off one of the invasion beaches.

6-99. Line of ships in the distance form Gooseberry breakwater. German obstructions are piled up on Omaha Beach following their removal.

GOOSEBERRIES-SHELTER BREAKWATER

The Gooseberries were artificial breakwaters off the beaches. Old merchant vessels in rows parallel with the beach formed the Gooseberry protective breakwaters (**6-98, 6-99,** and **6-100**).

THE GREAT STORM

Just when all concerned could congratulate themselves that, although schedules had not been met, combat losses and consumption of matériel had been less than expected, nature struck with the worst storm in almost half a century. "The Great Storm," as those who experienced it named the gale, seemed determined to prove that man and his artifacts were quite puny despite their best efforts.

Weather conditions that previously had exceeded all

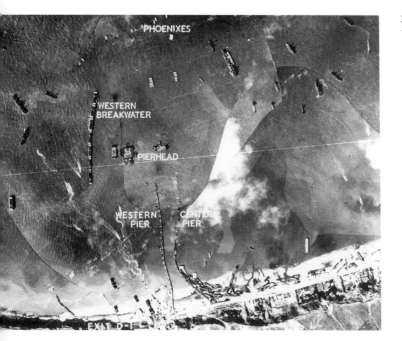

6-100.   Aerial photo of Mulberry under construction at one of the American beaches. The Gooseberry breakwater does not show in the photo.

6-101. Waves batter a Mulberry harbor during the Great Storm. The ship at right is the old British battleship *Centurion,* sunk to serve as a breakwater and as an AA emplacement.

reasonable expectations for many days, began to deteriorate after 14 June. Finally, early on the morning of 19 June, a northeasterly gale began to rip through the artificial harbors erected at Normandy. By 1500, wind gusts of force seven were recorded along with 8-foot waves sweeping through the anchorages. Under this battering, Mulberry A at Omaha Beach began to disintegrate. Mulberry B in the British sector held up much better; parts of it were still in position years later (**6-101**).

All unloading ceased during the afternoon of 19 June, with all craft seeking shelter behind the Gooseberries. At high tide, the waves were breaking over the lines of sunken ships. Undoubtedly they saved numerous craft from destruction in the British sector, but both Gooseberries in the American area lost their protective value. About thirty landing craft broke loose from their moorings and crashed into the piers and Rhinos (**6-102**). The pier was completely wrecked, with five Phoenix caissons lost and two-thirds of the detached breakwater destroyed (**6-103**).

Yet despite the appalling, disheartening devastation, within two days men and matériel were flowing in again in impressive numbers.

6-102. Landing vessels, battered by the storm, crash into the piers.

6-103. Twisted remains of the beachhead bridge at Omaha Beach following the storm.

CHAPTER 7 | Cherbourg

The early capture of Cherbourg was an integral part of the Overlord plan. To liberate France, not to mention moving on to occupy Germany, would require access to a major seaport, and Cherbourg was the best in the area. Had there been the slightest question of the need for a permanent harbor through which to funnel men and matériel, the Great Storm provided the answer. The temporary anchorages, however ingenious, were much too fragile to depend upon now that the initial landings had been made.

The need to take Cherbourg as rapidly as possible was the Allies' major concern. By 21 June, a day before the Great Storm had abated, Major General Collins, commander of VII Corps, issued orders to his divisional commanders to make the drive toward Cherbourg and its capture now their top priorities (7-1).

Well aware of Cherbourg's strategic significance to the Allies, the Germans were grimly determined to defend it. By 18 June, an American drive to the west across Cotentin peninsula, led by Maj. Gen. Louis A. Craig's 9th Division, had cut off German forces in the peninsula from the rest of the Wehrmacht. Although trapped, the Germans were resolved to thwart the American effort to capture the French port.

Commanding the Cherbourg garrison was General-leutnant von Schlieben of the 709th Division. Hitler had ordered him to make the city and its environs an impregnable fortress. In this object, the nearby rugged terrain was an asset, being readily defensible. In the city, von Schlieben had some forty thousand troops and had issued orders "to shoot on sight anyone leaving his post because of cowardice."

From 19–20 June, the divisions of Collins's VII Corps swept northward toward Cherbourg, only to be stopped dead in their tracks at the Germans' outer defense perimeter—a system of fortifications spanning an area seven miles west, four miles south, and eight miles east of Cherbourg. On 22 June, the VII Corps—by now numbering six divisions, including the 82d and 101st Airborne—stood ready to take up the advance toward its objective.

Collins, however, realized that his forces would need help. On 23 June he signaled to Rear Admiral Deyo (Force "U" Bombardment Force) that, in view of the strength of the German positions, he needed naval bombardment quickly—the next day if possible. But many of Deyo's vessels were either in Portland or en route there. Thus, earliest possible date for the naval gunfire to commence was 25 June.

In the meantime, Collins moved three of his divisions into position for the final assault on Fortress Cherbourg—9th on the left, 79th in the center, and 4th on the right, pressing the Germans farther and farther in toward the city. Photo 7-2 shows a portion of the town of Valognes, as it appeared on 24 June, after the 313th Infantry Regiment of Collins's 79th Division had passed through.

Deyo's bombardment force, augmented by heavy units

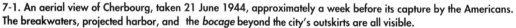

7-1. An aerial view of Cherbourg, taken 21 June 1944, approximately a week before its capture by the Americans. The breakwaters, projected harbor, and the *bocage* beyond the city's outskirts are all visible.

7-2. Center of the town of Valognes on 24 June, in the wake of the 313th Infantry Regiment, 79th Division. Note the jeep nicknamed "Always Ruth" and the trucks and power equipment already at work clearing the rubble.

7-3. USS *Quincy* (CA-71) lobs a salvo from number III turret past the cruiser HMS *Glasgow* (*right*).

from Force "O," left Portland at 0430 on 25 June in two groups: Group 1, which included the battleship *Nevada*, heavy cruisers *Tuscaloosa* and *Quincy*, and British cruisers HMS *Glasgow* and *Enterprise*; and under Rear Admiral Bryant, Group 2, which boasted battleships *Texas* and *Arkansas*. As the combined force neared the French coast, Collins requested that the Navy deliver "call fire" only, to minimize the chances of Americans being hit by their own shells.

Shortly after noon on 25 June, the bombardment began.

The following series of photos shows some of the fire support action. Here *Quincy* fires past *Glasgow*. The time of this photo is uncertain. Likely it was taken during the duel with battery "308" between Querqueville and Cherbourg, but before 1251, when two 150mm shells struck *Glasgow* and set it afire (7-3).

Having been almost destroyed at Pearl Harbor, *Nevada*

seemed bent on proving that it had paid its dues and hence-forth was invulnerable. At 1212 it commenced firing at a target near Tonneville, a village two miles west of Cherbourg (7-4 and 7-5). The Germans did not take the bombardment tamely. In photo 7-6 a shell lands quite near *Quincy*'s bow.

While Deyo's Force 1 battled the German batteries west of Cherbourg, Rear Admiral Bryant's ships took on the strongest of the German batteries near Cherbourg—"Battery Hamburg" (7-7). *Arkansas* opened the engagement with a salvo at 1208. Other German batteries in the vicinity also returned fire. Two American destroyers, *Barton* (DD-722) and *Laffey* (DD-724), were the first ships that Battery Hamburg struck.

After being straddled repeatedly by German shell fire, *Texas* finally sustained two hits, the first at 1234 (7-8) on the port bow in a compartment below the wardroom. At 1316 a shell hit the top of the conning tower (7-9).

The bombardment ended at 1501 when Deyo signaled Bryant to return to Portland. Von Schlieben gave the Allied naval endeavor high marks, saying that the heavy Allied bombardment from the sea had made him realize that resistance was useless. Admiral Krancke also felt that the action was definitely a contributing factor in the loss of Cherbourg.

On 26 June, the 4th and 79th divisions entered the city (7-10). Fighting was bitter, with the Germans resisting street by street and house by house. The campaign cost the Americans 2,800 killed and 13,500 wounded. The capture of Cherbourg is often considered the end of the Normandy campaign.

7-4. *Nevada*, of Force Group 1, shells German shore batteries near Cherbourg.

7-5. Guns of *Nevada*'s number IV turret belch flame and smoke during the bombardment of targets west of Cherbourg.

7-6. Seen from the cruiser's bridge, German shells splash off *Quincy*'s bow during the bombardment. Note 20mm AA mounts on the bow.

7-7. The duel with "Battery Hamburg." Enemy fire falls far short during the *Texas*'s battle with the four German 288mm guns located near Fermanville, six miles east of Cherbourg.

7-8. A German 240mm dud that struck *Texas* at 1234. Rear Admiral Bryant and Capt. Charles A. Baker stand guard over the trophy.

7-9. German shells fall within 200 yards of *Texas*, now joined by *Arkansas*, the ship from which this photograph was taken.

7-10. Cherbourg during 26 June, seen from one of the concrete pillboxes overlooking the city. An Army major is in the foreground, and the harbor facilities are off in the distance.

7-11. Generalleutnant von Schlieben steps ashore in England as a POW subsequent to his surrender on 26 June.

7-12. Americans blow up a pillbox during the final assaults on Cherbourg during 28 June. Note the concertina wire in the foreground.

7-13. Near one of the city's fortifications, German POWs from Cherbourg await transfer to POW camps on 28 June. The American guards at left appear curiously nonchalant.

On 25 June von Schlieben had radioed headquarters, "Loss of this city shortly is unavoidable." After receiving word of the naval attack, he concluded that further sacrifices would be futile. But Hitler had ordered that Cherbourg be defended "until the last cartridge," and Rommel had to pass on this unrealistic order. After advising that he had burned documents and destroyed codes, von Schlieben surrendered (**7-11**). Hard fighting continued even after he gave up, partly because of fanatical die-hard resistance, and partly because von Schlieben was out of communication with a substantial portion of his troops (**7-12**).

Thus, many of the Germans who had defended Cherbourg marched off into captivity (**7-13** and **7-14**). For them the war was over. Evidently at least one Frenchman was happy to see them go, as he stands at attention for "The Star-Spangled Banner" (**7-15**).

7-14. German troops march through the streets of Cherbourg and into captivity for the duration of the war. Note the carbine carried by the American captain at the head of the column and the man armed with a pistol on the right.

7-15. A French civilian stands at attention alongside the American battalion commander during the playing of "The Star-Spangled Banner" in Cherbourg on 28 June.

7-16. VII Corps commander, Major General Collins, describes to Lieutenant General Bradley how the corps took Cherbourg.

Some parts of the post-capture period had their pleasant moments. Undoubtedly Collins took satisfaction in praising his men's exploits to Bradley (7-16). In a gesture of gratitude repeated innumerable times during the liberation of France, a young French woman bestowed a kiss upon Major General Barton (7-17).

The Eisenhowers, father and son, visited the Isigny region about this time, and John mentioned to Bradley the difference in attitude of the locals from what he had observed at Bayeux earlier. Smiling, Bradley replied, "John, the people are now convinced that the Allies are here to stay."

The Germans had not gone gently out of Cherbourg. In accordance with Hitler's wishes, they left the city, and particularly its port facilities, a mass of burned, twisted wreckage. They demolished docks and scuttled cargo vessels (7-18). Other damage, of course, was the result of the fight-

7-17. Major General Barton, commander of the 4th Infantry Division during the Cherbourg campaign, receives a kiss from a young French woman.

7-18. View of *Gare Maritime*, the railway ferry terminal in Cherbourg harbor, showing the work of German demolition teams.

7-19. Cherbourg Railway Station, where a collapsed section of roof pins a freight car to the track.

ing itself (**7-19** and **7-20**). Evidence of German demolition also appears in photo **7-21**.

Of particular satisfaction to the British was the capture of an incomplete V-1 launching site (**7-22** and **7-23**). The camouflage netting, conduit, and reinforced concrete rods indicate further construction was anticipated.

Before Cherbourg could be used as a harbor, German mines had to be cleared from the area outside the harbor. Twenty American minesweepers and two flotillas of British craft were allocated for this purpose (**7-24**). Similar "sweeping" efforts had to be conducted on land as well (**7-25**), because the Germans left Cherbourg a nightmarish, booby-trapped ruin (**7-26**). After the actual capture of the city, another three weeks of difficult, dangerous, and intensive salvage work was required before the Allies could begin to use the port of Cherbourg.

7-20. A damaged German gun emplacement in the fortifications near Cherbourg harbor. Camouflage netting hangs in ruins.

7-22. Incomplete German V-1 launching site near Cherbourg on 12 July, with a view of the rear of the launch ramp.

7-21. View of Slipway Number 1 on 4 July, looking toward *Basin Napoleon III*. The old cannons are used as bollards.

7-23. Front view of the V-1 launch ramp; note staff car at right. Camouflage netting at left appears to be hiding some additional construction materials.

7-24. Two British minesweepers detonate German mines in the waters off Cherbourg just before a convoy of supply ships enters during 2 July. Fort L'Ouest is in the background.

7-25. American Army engineers work to disable a live mine found underneath the docks at Cherbourg.

7-26. An American 2-8-0 "Consolidation" locomotive swings out from the SS *Seatrain Texas* and is placed upon rails on 13 July 1944. This was part of the effort to replace French rolling stock destroyed during the fighting and by German demolition teams, whose work Hitler later commended as "exemplary."

CHAPTER 8 | Aftermath

By 1 July, the Cotentin peninsula had been liberated. The tide of battle swept onward, leaving behind it bits and pieces of history curiously like the flotsam found in the wake of any storm-induced, unnatural high tide. The victory had come at a terrible cost to the inhabitants. Hundreds of thousands of Frenchmen were displaced, maimed, or killed in the fighting to liberate Normandy. Americans felt a special obligation to alleviate their suffering. As always with American troops, the children were treated with particular care and attention. Almost any GI with candy in his possession was sure to share it, or give it outright, to a child as hungry for his kindness as for the sweet (8-1).

Wrecked and abandoned German positions and weapons littered the landscape. The pillbox in photo 8-2, located on Omaha Beach, took a direct hit above its guns. Photo 8-3, taken at the same time as 8-2, shows damage to the muzzle break of the same gun.

Such impaired armaments could provide valuable clues in assessing the effectiveness of the American fire. In photo 8-4, a soldier uses a Strateline ruler to estimate damage to a German turret at Utah Beach. This turret sustained considerable impact damage and a large number of hits in a small area. There can be little doubt that the resultant concussion alone would have been enough to kill the occupants.

The children, of course, found other uses for the enemy's wrecked weapons. In a particularly poignant scene (8-5), two children play among discarded German rifles, machine pistols, helmets, and mess gear. Are they brother and sister, or strangers thrown together in the movement of refugees? In any case, the scars carried by this generation of youngsters went beyond the physical.

The work of interring the dead proceeded apace. The American resting in this lonely, shallow grave awaits reburial in a large cemetery with his countrymen killed in the Normandy campaign. The box of machine-gun ammunition in the foreground is a grim reminder—as if any were needed—that this was no natural death (8-6). In photo 8-7, two French peasants have brought flowers and a prayer to a fallen American soldier. There is a certain tenderness in their attitudes and expressions that makes one wonder if this couple, like so many of their countrymen, has lost a son in this war.

The possibility always existed that among the papers the Germans left behind might be something of military value. So these items were carefully sought out and evaluated. The bulk of the Seventh Army's official written records, however, were either accidentally or deliberately destroyed following the disintegration of Germany's defenses in Normandy. Nevertheless, the retreating Germans

8-1. A U.S. medical corpsman gives candy to a French girl injured in the invasion.

8-2. A German 88mm gun protrudes from a battered pillbox on Omaha Beach. This photo was taken on 4 August 1944.

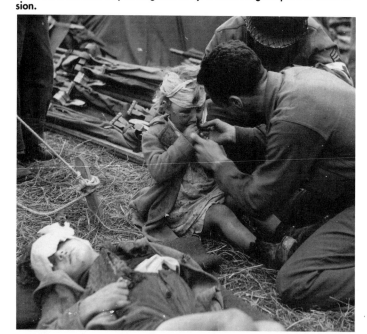

8-3. Damage to the muzzle break of the gun in photo 8-2.

8-4. A soldier holds up his Strateline ruler to document damage to this German turret in the Utah Beach fortifications.

8-5. Children playing with debris left behind by the retreating German Army.

8-6. A dead American soldier rests in a temporary grave, awaiting disinterment and reburial in the large cemetery.

8-7. French peasants pay their respects to an American who met with his death far from home.

8-8. Army officers examine papers left behind in a pillbox along the Normandy coast.

left behind vast quantities of materials and papers, and these had to be sifted, sorted, and analyzed (**8-8**). This job continued until well after the war ended.

Some time during 13 July, PFC Michael Rolish of Johnstown, Pennsylvania, found a moment to relax. He had been on the move without rest since D-Day and had had neither the time nor, presumably, the inclination for a shave and haircut. Now one can almost hear his "Aaah!" of relief as he slips off his shoes and socks. The weapon in the holster to his right is a .45-caliber APC (**8-9**).

Germans continued to surrender, either in groups or, as in the case of this NCO, singly (**8-10**). He got his point across even though the small Nazi flag he carries is not exactly the usual instrument of surrender. In fact, his whole appearance is unorthodox. He wears lace-up boots and leggings instead of jackboots, an M1943 cap in place of a helmet, and his tunic flaps open over suspenders and pants that ride up much too high on his torso.

Processing prisoners was somewhat complicated by the large numbers of wounded. The man on the stretcher in photo **8-11** is suffering from a neck wound. As indicated by the bit of aluminum braid on his shoulder strap, the man bearing the right rear corner of the stretcher is an NCO candidate. The mixture of headgear—helmets, forage (overseas) caps, and M1943 caps—hints that standard wear was in short supply.

The German soldiers being processed in photo **8-12** seem to be taking their lot in good part. At least two are smiling, and they have their paybooks at the ready for identification. These men wear a mix of uniform. The third man in line on the right wears a service tunic with pleated pockets, a type in use earlier. With the need for simpler manufacturing methods, the Germans developed a service tunic without pleats, which most of the pictured soldiers are wearing.

Some prisoners were rounded up as early as D-Day. On Utah Beach, an enclosure of concertina wire and straight barbed wire surrounds a small group of POWs. An M-5A1 Stuart light tank with "breather" gear is in the background, along with a group of black American soldiers (**8-13**).

8-9. PFC Michael Rolish takes a rare moment to relax and take off his shoes.

8-10. A German NCO is brought in at the point of a bayonet.

8-11. German POWs bear a stricken comrade to a landing craft waiting on the beach at Normandy.

8-12. German soldiers being searched and questioned in an encampment on the Normandy beachhead.

8-13. Resting in an enclosure on Utah Beach, German prisoners await transport to camps in England. This photo was taken on 6 June 1944.

The large number of prisoners entailed special logistics problems, such as furnishing adequate food. The group of Germans shown in photo 8-14 seem to be enjoying a meal of U.S. Army K rations, which may say something about the quality of their own commissariat. Evidently whoever was in charge of POWs at Omaha Beach had a lot to learn, for two of the Germans brandish open knives. Fortunately they seem to be focused only on the food.

8-14. Captured Germans "feast" on K rations on Omaha Beach during 9 June.

8-15. A forlorn group of German POWs trudges to the transports that will carry them to England.

8-16. Italian and German prisoners on board *Texas* being taken to camps in England during June 1944.

8-17. German POWs disembark from an LCT at a port somewhere in England.

Soon these prisoners and others like them would board transports taking them to England for the duration (**8-15**). Even battleships were pressed into this service. The POWs' stay on the wet sands of Normandy may have been miserable; but for many, seasickness on board the heaving, rolling ships was worse, as evidenced by the seasick individuals sprawled on *Texas*'s deck (**8-16**).

The English Channel has been notorious for centuries for its uncomfortable passage, and these men may well have been glad to see land—even enemy land—as they disembarked at an unnamed port in England. Here no one was taking chances, and guards stood by armed with Sten submachine guns. The soldier at far left is a *gefreiter* (private first class) radioman, evidenced by his specialty badge. There has been some effort to segregate the NCOs into the line nearest the camera, there being gefreiters, obergefreiters, unteroffiziers, and NCO/officer candidates. The third man in line from the left even carries his own beer stein (**8-17**).

In the aftermath of the initial campaign, high-level discussions took place. Eisenhower met with Montgomery to talk over the new attacks launched against the Wehrmacht (**8-18** and **8-19**). In the latter photo, one of Montgomery's dogs, either "Hitler" or "Rommel," stands at attention in the background.

As was his custom, Ike took the opportunity to chat with men of lesser rank, in this case Flying Officer A. K. Asboe of Brisbane, Australia. The pilot's uniform has definitely seen better days: the rank insignia on his shoulder strap is coming unstitched, and the badge on his cap is ready to fall off. But no chewing-out is portended. Eisenhower's face shows only friendly amusement (**8-20**).

8-18. Montgomery's personal (U.S.) C-47 rests on the hardstand at a fighter base in Normandy on 19 July 1944. As the sign indicates, this was a special parking place for aircraft belonging to four-star generals.

8-19. Montgomery meets with Eisenhower following the initial campaign.

8-20. During this meeting, Eisenhower chats with one of the RAF pilots of his fighter escort for the flight to France.

When women were first accepted into the armed forces, first as auxiliaries, then as full-fledged members, many a diehard predicted at least the end of civilization as they knew it. Some never did become reconciled. But the women proved their worth, and by mid-July 1944, with the fighting over along the beachheads, the number of servicewomen in France began to grow rapidly. In photo **8-21**, two GIs and two WACs (Women's Army Corps) look over their French texts. While this particular photo is obviously posed, there is no reason to suppose that the quartet, and many like them, were not serious about their studies.

The booklets they are holding appear to be examples of the little technical manuals the War Department issued. These did not pretend to make one fluent in the language, but mastery of the contents could enable them to ask directions, order a meal, and conduct a simple conversation. Perhaps most valuable, this smattering could convince the natives that one was well-disposed toward them.

On 15 July, the first WACs arrived in France. In photo **8-22** we see them preparing to jump from their transport into an LCM.

Nurses, of course, had preceded the WACs. First to arrive were members of the 13th Field Hospital, shown here eating from their mess kits. They appear to be enjoying their alfresco meal (**8-23**).

8-22. The first WACs to arrive in France disembark from a transport and pile into an LCM on 15 July.

8-21. A sergeant and a technical 5th grade study French with two members of the Women's Army Corps (WACs) while crossing the English Channel during 15 July 1944.

8-23. Field nurses of the 13th Field Hospital, the first to arrive in Normandy, enjoy one of many meals in the field.

8-24. Military life begins to return to normal, 17 July 1944.

8-25. Soldiers eat and listen to the latest news on their Philco radio outside their pup tents on the Normandy beachhead, 12 June.

8-26. Cpl. Charles Vaughn, a barber from Lush, Wyoming, opens up shop in Normandy.

8-27. Two USO performers, Stephanie Dale and Josephine Del Mar, step out of the "Ladies only" facilities at the show on 25 July.

Even more than the presence of women, the burgeoning of rules and regulations attested to the fact that normalcy was setting in. This list of fines was a daunting welcome for anyone entering the particular area (8-24). By today's standards these fines are nominal; but in terms of 1944 military pay, they represented a formidable slice of a man's salary.

Men not engaged in pushing the Germans soon began searching for recreation to battle the resulting boredom. The radio was a staple in this quest, not only bringing them entertainment but keeping them reasonably posted on what was happening in the outside world. In this photo (8-25) the soldier on the right has come up with some "real" food as opposed to government issue.

Another indication of a return to something like normalcy was the concern with personal appearance. Hence Cpl. Charles Vaughn found ready customers for his "Tonsorial Shoppe." On the Fourth of July, 1944, one of Vaughn's customers was Cpl. John P. Britz (8-26).

The USO (United Service Organization) was not long in responding to the men's longing for entertainment from home. On 25 and 26 July, the first camp show in France played to a "full house" (8-27 and 8-28). As in their home-

towns, men found the movies a cornerstone of the recreational scene. Any movie offered usually drew a good audience, regardless of the film's merit. *Casanova Brown* was probably par for the course (**8-29**). The story had been screened twice before as *Little Accident,* and certainly was not up to the talents of superstar Gary Cooper and the gifted Teresa Wright, but who was complaining?

Of course the Red Cross was in evidence. On 24 August the organization visited Omaha Beach, setting up a "Clubmobile," to the evident satisfaction of a group of Seabees (**8-30**).

Perhaps the most convincing evidence that Hitler and his Nazis were finished in Normandy appears in this record of an open-air Jewish worship service (**8-31**), with a jeep pressed into service as an altar.

8-28. American soldiers crowd around an improvised stage at the first USO camp show in France on 26 July 1944.

8-30. Navy Seabees take a break in their routine for some refreshments. Note the fresh flowers on the vehicle's counter at right.

8-29. Army nurses and servicemen line up on 8 August for an almost first-run movie, *Casanova Brown,* starring Gary Cooper and Teresa Wright.

8-31. Jewish services proceed in Normandy quite unhindered on the shores of Hitler's "Fortress Europe."

CHAPTER 9 | Epilogue

Burial of the dead, with dignity and as expeditiously as possible, was an ongoing and distressing part of the pattern of war. Every attempt was made to identify the fallen men. As unpleasant, indeed as heartbreaking, as it was to inform parents or wives that their sons or husbands had been killed, it was much worse to have to report them missing. Death carried its own finality; uncertainty never ended. Hence the services issued the metal identification tags that the GI called "dog tags" and was supposed to wear at all times.

This view of an early burial grounds, taken on 12 June 1944, shows that the site, although temporary, was neat and orderly. Whenever possible the dog tags of the dead had been affixed to the small wooden markers for identification (9-1).

Approximately two weeks later, Chaplain Paul J. McGovern led a group of combat engineers in prayer at the same site. A good number of men have turned out for the

9-1. American troops present arms in tribute to their fallen comrades who lie buried in a temporary cemetery on the beachhead at Omaha Beach, 12 June 1944.

9-2. On 25 June 1944, Chaplain Paul J. McGovern leads a group of combat engineers in prayer during a memorial service at the temporary cemetery on Omaha Beach.

9-3. French civilians and some German POWs work on construction of the permanent cemetery on Omaha Beach, 4 August 1944.

service, and their attitude is reverent. Two signs of the times appear in this photo: Two barrage balloons hover in the distance, and a motion picture cameraman grinds away at far right (9-2).

As soon as practicable, work began on permanent cemeteries, employing French civilians and in some cases German POWs. In photo 9-3, taken on Omaha Beach on 4 August 1944, temporary "lean-to" wooden crosses are being erected in the background. In photo 9-4 we see these workers setting crosses in place on the graves.

By the time a year had rolled around, such cemeteries had begun to take on a look of peace and tranquility. The burial ground at Ste.-Mère Église on 1 June 1945, just after the final Allied victory in Europe, could be any similar site in the United States, well sodded and with the graves decorated with little American flags. In the third row, a Star of David among the crosses shows that a Jewish serviceman is buried among his Christian comrades (9-5).

In contrast, an aerial view of the great Normandy cemetery taken on 28 May 1957, gives an awesome impression, almost impersonal in its size (9-6). The human touch returns, however, as two men stand with heads bowed among graves decorated with flowers (9-7).

There is something inexpressibly sad and touching about such military cemeteries, much different from the gentle melancholy most community burial grounds engender. In the latter, most of the gravestones indicate that those resting there have lived out full lives. Some untimely deaths are recorded, but they are few. In the cemeteries such as those in Normandy, all the occupants were cut down before their time. Not only were these young people deprived of life, but civilization was deprived of them. Perhaps beneath one of these crosses or stars lies the genius who could have found a cure for cancer, composed great symphonies, or written immortal poetry. And almost all of them could have enriched the world with lives of unobtrusive worth.

One can only be grateful for their sacrifices, which helped deliver a continent from unspeakable horrors. May no such sacrifice ever be required again.

9-4. In the background of the previous photo, French workers set crosses upon the graves of the slain American soldiers.

9-5. Ste.-Mère-Église Cemetery, 1 June 1945.

9-6. Aerial view of the Normandy Cemetery, 28 May 1957.

9-7. Two men pay tribute to the fallen.

The Wall of Liberty

Among the many events and ceremonies commemorating the fiftieth anniversary of the 6 June 1944 D-Day invasion, perhaps none will have the permanence or serve as well as the Wall of Liberty. The Battle of Normandy Foundation is responsible for building the world's first monument to honor American veterans, men and women, living and deceased, who served in the European theater of operations during World War II. Rising near the invasion beaches in Caen, Normandy, it will serve as a lasting remembrance of American contributions in restoring liberty and democracy to the continent of Europe.

The Wall of Liberty will stand as a true testament to one of America's greatest strengths—its spirit of volunteerism. Private citizens and corporations are contributing to ensure that American World War II European theater of operations veterans will have their names etched in the Wall of Liberty for tomorrow's generations to view and remember.

Ground-breaking ceremonies for the Wall of Liberty will be held on 6 June 1994, with the first section of the wall scheduled to be completed on 8 May 1995, the fiftieth anniversary of VE-Day. Registrations will remain open after that date. For further information or to register a veteran, write to the Battle of Normandy Foundation, 1730 Rhode Island Avenue, N.W., Suite 612, Washington, D.C. 20036, or call 1–800–WW2–VETS.

Equivalent Officer Ranks

U.S.	German Army and Air Force	German Waffen-SS
None	Reichsmarschall	*None*
General of the Army	Generalfeldmarschall	Reichsführer-SS
General	Generaloberst	Oberstgruppenführer
Lieutenant general	General der	Obergruppenführer
Infantry	Infanterie	
Artillery	Artillerie	
Mountain troops	Gebirgstruppen	
Cavalry	Kavallerie	
Signals	Nachrichtentruppen	
Armor	Panzertruppen	
Engineers	Pioniere	
Air Force	Flieger	
Paratroopers	Fallschirmtruppen	
Antiaircraft artillery	Flakartillerie	
Air Force signals	Luftnachrichtentruppen	
Major general	Generalleutnant	Gruppenführer
Brigadier general	Generalmajor	Brigadeführer
None	None	Oberführer
Colonel	Oberst	Standartenführer
Lieutenant colonel	Oberstleutnant	Obersturmbannführer
Major	Major	Sturmbannführer
Captain	Hauptmann	Haupsturmführer
Captain (Cavalry)	Rittmeister	
First lieutenant	Oberleutnant	Obersturmführer
Second lieutenant	Leutnant	Unterstrumführer

Credits

All photographs, unless otherwise noted below, are courtesy of the National Archives of the United States.

Army War College: 2-20, 2-21, 5-11, 8-5

Bundesarchiv: 1-31, 1-33, 2-1, 2-8, 2-14, 2-15, 2-16

Maxwell Air Force Base: 1-22, 3-30 through 3-37, 4-30 through 4-33, 5-74, 5-76 through 5-79, 6-6, 6-7, 6-13, 6-16 through 6-19, 6-41 through 6-44, 6-100

Naval Historical Center: 1-7, 1-19, 1-20, 5-43, 6-33, 7-6, 7-7

Samuel L. Sox, Jr.: 2-60, 2-61

Smithsonian: 5-75, 6-5, 6-14

Index

Numbers in italics indicate page contains a corresponding photograph

About the Authors

Donald M. Goldstein, Lieutenant Colonel, USAF (Ret.), is professor of public and international affairs at the University of Pittsburgh. **Katherine V. Dillon,** Chief Warrant Officer, USAF (Ret.), of Arlington, Virginia, collaborated with Dr. Goldstein and the late Dr. Gordon W. Prange on eight best-selling books, including *At Dawn We Slept, Miracle at Midway,* and the Brassey's publications *God's Samurai: Lead Pilot at Pearl Harbor* (1990) and *The Pearl Harbor Papers* (1993). **J. Michael Wenger** is a freelance historian living in Raleigh, North Carolina. He worked with Goldstein and Dillon on Brassey's *The Way It Was: Pearl Harbor—The Original Photographs* (1991).